Everyday Heroes

A Collection of
Inspirational & Motivational Stories
From Around the World

COMPILED BY MATT BACAK

DEDICATION

Dedicated to the Heroes of tomorrow. Proceeds from this book go directly to Children's Healthcare of Atlanta.

TABLE OF CONTENTS

ACKNOWLEDGMENTS

Thank you to all of the authors who shared their stories in this book, and a special thank you to the people on my team who came together to make this book a great success!

-Matt Bacak

INTRODUCTION

I want to begin by telling you a story. This is about a man who was a huge success, who made his first million right out of college, and who then built that into a thriving business and a life style most of us dream about. He had 15 thriving companies. A big house. A happy family. And the belief that nothing could take that away from him.

Until one December day in 2008 he heard a knock on the door. Two men in black suits stood in front of him. And then they said the five words that can terrify even the strongest person:

"We're with the Internal Revenue."

They came into his house, sat him down, and began to ask him questions. Questions about his business. His finances. His associates. His family.

He answered whatever they asked, until finally he said, "Why do you want to know all this?"

"We can't tell you that," they said.

"Well, have I done something wrong?"

"We can't tell you that," they said.

"But if you just tell me what this is about, I'll do whatever I can to fix it. But I've got to know what you think I did."

"We can't tell you that."

Finally he realized he'd better shut up and get a lawyer before he said the wrong thing. He asked them to leave.

"Fine," they said. "But you should know that our investigation could result in your ending up in prison for five years."

So he hired a big tax lawyer, and then 12 of the top auditors in the country, who combed through the books of all his companies. None of them could find anything wrong, or any clue as to what brought the IRS down on this guy.

Over the next several months his life became a living hell. Concentrating on anything was almost impossible. His wife was close to a nervous breakdown. His kids didn't know why things at home had changed. And every day he wondered if this was the day he'd be carted off to prison.

And then one morning in April, 2009, a letter arrived. When he saw the IRS logo on the envelope his hands started to shake.

"You are no longer subject of a criminal investigation by our office.... However, this does not preclude re-entry by Criminal Investigation into this investigation."

He showed the letter to his expensive attorney, who said, "In all my years of practice, I've only ever seen two of these. What you have here is a Golden Ticket. With this you can get out from under this entire ordeal.

"However," he said, "This is not a GET OUT OF JAIL FREE card. They could come after you again any time they want, with no warning, and no more explanation than you got this time. The question is, are you willing to do whatever it takes to make sure that this never happens to you and your family again?"

"I'll do anything," he said.

"Then," his lawyer told him, "you're going to have to lose EVERYTHING. You'll have to bankrupt all your businesses. Cut all your business ties. And stop doing everything you're currently doing. You can't be associated with anything the IRS might have been investigating. In other words," his lawyer said, "YOU'RE GOING TO HAVE TO START OVER FROM NOTHING."

This was NOT what he wanted to hear. He was mad. He was depressed. And he was scared. But he had no choice.

"Just one condition," he told his lawyer. "I won't leave my merchants and my employees holding the bag, no matter what."

So dipping into his own pocket, he paid everyone what he owed them, bankrupt all 15 of his companies, and said goodbye to his wealth, his career and his livelihood. He was finally free, and he was broke.

And one more thing you should know. This guy I've been talking about – it's me.

This entire story is absolutely true. In 2008 the IRS came after me, even though to this day they have never found anything amiss in any of my businesses, and they have never said what it was they were investigating.

I tell you this story because I want you to know that when this all happened, when I lost everything, I was where many of you are right now: with a burning desire to take care of my family, to create a good life for them, to have a nice home and to give my kids a good future. But I had no business and no savings – nothing but my credit cards. And I wasn't even allowed to go back to what I had done before.

But I did have one thing going for me: I knew from my previous success that the Internet was a gold mine waiting to be tapped, if I could just figure out how. So I searched and searched until I found a hero. Hopefully, after reading this you'll find one too!

Enjoy the book!

Matt Bacak

SECTION 1:

OVERCOMING FEAR

FACE YOUR FEAR, FORTUNE IS NEAR

BRIAN T. EVANS JR.

Growing up as a child and a young adult were scary years for me, personally. Every two or three years my parents moved my sister and I to a different state because of my father's job. This was very hard for me because each time we moved I was forced into a new school where I had to learn to make friends all over again, and say goodbye to my old ones. I do believe that I hid my fears from others pretty well, but this doesn't change the underlying fact that for way too long I let my fears get the best of me mentally at a young age. Therefore, looking back on that part of my life and comparing it to parts of my life today, I believe that fear is one of, if not the most powerful of all the negative emotions that you can experience in the world. It does nothing but cause endless pain and suffering to the person that is afraid.

A year after graduating from college and landing a job on Wall Street, it would seem as though life was going very well for me. However, in my mind it wasn't. I had a safe job making a decent salary, but life didn't feel right to me. I felt as though I was missing out on better opportunities that the world had to offer, but I was very afraid to make a change.

Until one day I got home after work and there was a package at my front doorstep. In the package was a book with a yellow post-it-note on the cover. The note said, "Son, read this…take notes…let's talk, Dad." The book was called "Retire Young Retire Rich," and of course I immediately started reading it. The main takeaway I got from that book was this:

Most people go through life working at a job and trying to save enough money so they can retire one day when they are 65 or 70 years old. The better way, according to the book, was to be the entrepreneur that owned a business with employees, rather than being an employee that worked for a business owner. Being the business owner is how you "Retire Young and Retire Rich."

After getting and reading this book, it completely changed the way I thought about life, and my future. I decided to face my fear, I quit my job in 2004, and I went out on my own to work for myself in the entrepreneurial world and I've never looked back since. I was scared to death but it turned out to be the best decision I've ever made (except for marrying my wife of course).

Looking back on my decision to quit my job, and dealing with all of the up and down days of entrepreneurship since then, here's what I would like to teach you, the reader, what I know about fear, because when you learn to face your fear, fortune is near!

Everybody in life encounters the emotion of fear. Fear is not a bad thing. It exists for our survival and protection as an early warning signal. But what you need to understand is that there is a very big difference between the healthy fear that alerts you of a harmful situation such as falling off a cliff, then there is to a fear that causes constraint, that causes anxiety, stress and keeps you from living your daily life to the fullest extent possible. Quite obviously, the fear that I will be focusing on with you is the latter.

Upon accepting the fact that you do have mental fears (yes you do, swallow your pride, it's ok) you must now determine what it is *exactly* that has a tendency to keep you awake at night...what is it *exactly* that causes this fear inside you? I challenge you to attempt to take a step back and look at yourself differently, almost as if you are looking at yourself while standing in someone else's shoes, watching your daily routines, critiquing your every life move. Be willing to look at yourself openly and subjectively and begin to identify exactly what it is that may be keeping you from living your life 100% on your terms. And then, once you start to understand and see the outside perspective view of what your fears are, what you then must do is dig deeper and try to understand and find the root of these fears. What is the underlying reason that may be causing these fears to occur inside of you?

Napoleon Hill, the author of *Think and Grow Rich,* once said, "Free yourself of fear and you free yourself of a man-made devil." There are two very important words that I want to discuss with you within this quote: "man-made." Think about this for a moment. The definition of man-made is: not of natural origin; prepared or made artificially. Therefore, most of your fears in life are man-made. You've "created" them. They are "artificial." You've brought them on yourself and the good news is you control the on/off switch!

It is also extremely important for you to know that fear is magnetic. Believe it or not, your fear is constantly attracting more fear everyday. It attracts more negative feelings, more negative pain, and more negative suffering. The more fear you have the more fear you're likely to attract. Now if that doesn't scare you, I don't know what does (sorry for the pun).

Here are some very important items to be aware of in regards to what fear actually does to you. It...
- Attracts more fear and negative emotions.
- Causes constraint, stress and anxiety.
- Causes mental paralysis.
- Affects your life; past, present, and future.
- Affects your relationships with your friends, family and loved ones.
- Keeps you from being truly happy.
- Causes dread, and regret.
- Robs you of courage to act effectively.
- And so much more.

Do any of these above items look or feel familiar to you in any way, shape, or form? If so, start by simply trying to recognize these feelings of fear that you encounter and when they occur so you can get in control and turn them off mentally. These are negative feelings blinding you from the truth of what life can really and truly hold for you once you are able to live a life of "no fear."

I personally believe it to be an absolute fact that your mind has limitless power to make your dreams come true (this is not a cliché, but rather an absolute fact) provided that you allow your mind to work free of fear. One of the many detrimental things about fear is it can and will do everything it possibly can to stop you before you get started. Fear has a complete imagination of its own, which is only influenced by negative emotions. If you let your fears take hold of you and constrain you, then all your ability to create and achieve will be crippled and potentially lost forever, all because of fear.

Do I personally encounter feelings of fear and anxiety in my business and life still today? Absolutely, *I am human just like you*. However, I've learned to recognize and understand the truth, that this fear is typically a subject of my own imagination. I make an effort daily to keep my state of mind going strong and stay positive and optimistic to prevent all the negative feelings and fears that could potentially come into my life and cause me to begin to falter. It is by no means easy. But just simply by you recognizing these feelings, it allows you to begin to overcome the problems and challenges and fears and negative feelings that can result from various negative situations.

A large part about having "no fear" is controlling your state of mind. Instead of waking up each day and fearing the worst, you need to start reaching and aspiring for the absolute best. Stop looking for symptoms that may cause you to fail, and begin looking for more ways that can cause you to succeed. Now, I'm not preaching to you that a simple state of mind is going to prevent negative feelings or problems occurring within your life. But your state of mind will help you to overcome all these obstacles that you encounter that are part of life.

Additionally, too many people fear the unknown or the what-ifs. But if you think about it this way, why cause yourself to worry about something that is uncontrollable to you in the first place? You shouldn't fear what you cannot control. Which also brings up a very good point about the importance and mental power of control. I strive and choose to be in control of everything I possible can when it comes to my businesses and my impact on others. For example, I work for myself because I choose to be in control of my life, my income, my vacations, what I spend my money on, etc. To me, it is in some form or fashion insane to let someone else (an employer perhaps) be in control of and dictate the income in my life. This is truly preposterous, is it not? There is no law that says you have to work a 9-5 job making a fixed salary no matter how hard you work, and only get 12 vacation days a year. Yet this is the mentality of the society in which we live.

Moreover, if you have to rid yourself of certain bad habits in order to eliminate and rise above your fears, then by all means do it. If you have to remove yourself from certain people in your life in order to rise above your fears then do it. If you are not doing things that allow you to be in control of all aspects of your life that you can physically control, then do it.

Nobody said this was going to be easy. But you very likely may have to take drastic steps to get rid of the venom that's poisoning your mind. You need to do whatever it takes to live a life with "no fear."

Do yourself a favor and consider this the next time you encounter a fear that's holding you back. Ask yourself "What's the worst that can happen?" If you are not doing something that you want to do, or think you should do because you feel a sense of fear, simply ask yourself, "If I go ahead and do this anyway, if I try to start a new business this year, what is the worst that could possibly happen from doing this act?"

If you ask yourself this question and you really analyze the potential outcomes that could occur you'll begin to discover that what seemed like the worst, really isn't that bad after all. And if you know that you truly can live with a worst-case scenario result then perhaps you should proceed with those actions.

However, if the worst that could happen is something that could potentially put you out of your marriage, out of your house, or keep you awake at night because of other extremely life altering outcomes then you *probably* shouldn't do it. Everybody has a gut instinct and a conscience; be willing to trust yours!

Know that your mind has limitless power to make a desire come true, to make your dreams come true, to achieve your financial fortunes and the choice is all 100% yours. The most successful people of all time have had to overcome obstacles and fears that you too feel on a regular basis. That's life! Recognize this, accept this, and be mature about the process.

There is a very real difference between simply wearing a t-shirt that says "no fear" and actually choosing to live your life by it!

Face your fear, fortune is near!

HOW EXPENSIVE IS YOUR EGO?

CHRIS HICKMAN

Remember that someone has always made a bigger mistake than you have and gotten through it. The famous hockey player Wayne Gretzky said you miss 100% of the shots you don't take. During Michael Jordan's career, he has missed over 9000 shots and 26 times he's missed the game-winning shot. He was also cut from his high school basketball team.

What makes people keep going despite failure? I believe one factor is a well-controlled ego. We all need a little ego to be ambitious enough to take risks large enough to make failure painful. Yet it is the ability to not let failure destroy our ambition that gives people the courage to keep going through the rough part and reach their goals.

The more of an ego you have, the more expensive it is to maintain it. By that, I mean that you have to divert extra time and energy into maintaining it rather than going after your goals. Feeling sorry for yourself, worrying about the future, or putting on an angry front won't help you reach your goals, but they will soothe an ego. It feels like you're doing something to make yourself feel better, but that energy could be put to better use. This is why I say maintaining an ego is expensive.

I'd like to share with you some strategies that I've found will reduce the amount of attention your ego needs:

Point 1 - You can live through more failure than you think.

Many decisions we make are based out of fear of failure and not looking bad in front of others. But if you've lived long enough and you look back on those situations, most of the fears that we had were not rational fears. Even if everything did fall apart, most of the time what actually happened didn't match what your brain said would happen. But your brain, trying to protect your ego, inflates your fears.

The next time you think about taking an action when you feel fear, write down on a piece of paper what is the absolute worst that can happen. Rate this consequence on a scale from a scale from 1 to 10 with 10 being you would die and 1 being it would be a slight inconvenience. Very rarely is that number even close to a 10. Many times it only feels like a 10 in that moment, but once the moment has passed it's much closer to a 1.

Next, write on another sheet of paper about how much success you'll feel if you succeed in the action you're scared of. Use the same scale from 1 to 10 with 10 being ultimate success and accomplishment and 1 being no change. If the number is close to 10 then you should take action to achieve it.

Take public speaking for example. Why do you think public speaking is feared far more than death? The average person would rather be in the casket than speaking the eulogy. You just have a very nervous feeling and your ego is telling you not to do it because you might make a mistake and look foolish. Yet if you think about it, have you ever really heard someone complain about a bad speaker, especially after time has passed?

Looking back on a speech, you may find that the pain is rather low on the scale. However, the gains from practicing public speaking can be quite high. Speakers who hone their abilities get better over time and can learn to command a room. Even if people don't remember a good motivational speech completely, most people will remember how it made them feel. We are so primed for speeches to be boring that a good speech is remembered fondly.

Point 2 - Look back on the event from the future

That point about how people forget things once time has passed? You can do that in advance and eliminate a lot of anxiety. I always like to ask myself a few questions when thinking about taking an action that could better myself but where I could also fail and look stupid.

1. Will this really matter to me if I fail in 1 century?
2. Will this really matter to me if I fail in 1 decade?
3. Will this really matter to me if I fail in 1 year?
4. Will this really matter to me if I fail in 1 month?
5. Will this really matter to me if I fail in 1 week?
6. Will this really matter to me if I fail in 1 day?

And yes, even…

7. Will this matter if I fail in 1 minute?

Most of the time the answer is no and when it is yes it's normally only yes to a minute a day or maybe a week. This stepping-down trick is a very powerful mental control technique. Most people can agree that our failures aren't going to matter a century from now. Unless you're quite young and reading this, chances are you'll be dead. By answering that question with a no, it opens a gap in the mind to consider that your failure might not matter in the grand scheme of things. Reducing the time scale from that new point of view can get your mind to relax and forget about the fear of failure.

Think about a time when you wanted to ask someone out on a date. In the moment, it felt like the end of the world. But if you look at the questions above and ask yourself will this matter, it really only matters for that minute or maybe a day. The worst that happens is the other person says no. If you let your ego prevent you from asking at all because of failure, it could cost you the person you might have a family with. If you really think about it, almost all of the important relationships in your life outside of family were made because someone took the first step and put their ego aside.

Or maybe you've had a business idea but failed to act on it because you were afraid of what others might think. Did you ever see that same idea come to market later and make millions? Let me tell you, this is a frustrating experience! But you can use the step-down technique to make your business anxiety manageable.

Stepping down your fear of failure this way is a way to gradually starve your ego of energy. This energy can then be put to better use.

Point 3 - Move towards your fear

When your ego kicks in and gives you the feeling that you should not be doing something, it's not just something to control. It's also a signal that what you're doing just might be the exact place you need to be focusing your efforts. Moving toward your fear and failing anyway can be quite powerful.

Martial artists know this well. Brazilian jiu-jitsu is a very tough sport. It takes on average about 10 years to go from a brand new white belt to a black belt. In most cases, the better person in jiu-jitsu is the one who has lost the most times. Think about that… the more successful athlete is the one with the most losses. Being able to put your ego aside is the only way to be able to progress in this sport to get to mastery.

Serial entrepreneurs also know the value of moving toward your fear again and again. There is a saying that failure is just another word for feedback. It's instructive, not destructive. If you can move into your fear and learn from your errors, you'll gain a surprising amount of power. And where does that power come from? From spending your time and energy on something other than maintaining your ego.

Your ego could be costing you a lot in terms of relationships, money and overall happiness. The hard part about your ego is it can disguise itself as fear of failure. These fears can seem quite rational at the time, but when we reflect back on the situation later it wasn't worth waiting.

Just think if Wayne Gretzky and Michael Jordan let their egos get in the way of their success. You would be thinking… who are those people?

Your ego might have been expensive in the past but how expensive will you let your ego be in the future?

OVERCOMING FEAR AND FAILURE ...GETTING BACK TO BASICS

BENJAMIN BRESSINGTON

I was dealing with that moment every entrepreneur dreads. The one where your business venture did not work out. The proof of life failed for multiple reasons. Leaving you realizing that you have nothing to show for the last few months but lessons. I was out months of time, and thousands of dollars I had invested. But this time it was worse.

I was sitting in a new country in which I had just moved too. It was -30 outside and the snow was piling up. I didn't really understand how cold it was because I moved from Brisbane, Australia to Calgary, Canada. The day I landed in Calgary there was 100 degrees Celsius difference, so I was still learning what cold was.

Standing at the baggage claim in board shorts feeling the draft through the airport doors was a lesson in itself. That's when you realize how much you don't know about what cold really is.

But back to this moment of failed business reality. The temperature just made the reality of the situation feel worse. It felt cold.

I felt more alone than ever sitting in the apartment. No friends yet. No family close by. No support group. And the support group I was creating really didn't want to know the truth, I was the new guy. That meant I was left all alone.

This left me sitting on the couch, with limited savings thinking about how I am going to survive in this new country. I had less than 3 weeks until the rent was due. No list, no leads, no prospects, no idea what I should do.

I could either continue to feel sorry for myself and run back to the family safety net in Australia. Or deal with this reality in Canada and learn something new about myself.

The one thing I knew is that I was resourceful and could hustle.

This meant I needed to get back to the basics and create an offer that people would respond too.

It was simple. Create an offer, hustle that offer from online ads, to local networking events and get connected with people.

At that time was attending 2 or 3 local events a day away where I could. To meet people and be seen by people.

This was not ideal but at the time I knew I just needed to find one client and then another.

I found clients and was able to create an agency from nothing that created the lifestyle I have today.

Your business does not need to be complicated. Your offer needs to be simple and fill a real need in the market.

But your reason why and the hustle that drives you out the door each day, or to pick up the phone needs to be real. That's what I had. At times all I had was the drive to make it work and work it out along the way. This hustle and drive is what I continue to use to wake me up each day on fire.

The basics of business are basics for a reason. But because they are basics it is easy to dismiss them our think you know better. Until you have the basics working don't innovate. Make the basics work for you then you have the freedom and time to innovate and create exciting new things.

Every time I complicated my business and failed to keep it simple things just slow down and get harder. Or just out right fail. This would result in me having to restart over and over again, losing traction and jumping to the next new thing.

You will notice this resistance in small ways. At first you will notice that deals take longer to close or the push to get the deal closed in the first place is just not there.

You will have people that are hot and ready and then they just fall of the edge of the earth. Then there are the other 100 things that will rob your focus and attention each day.

The challenge of doing busy work rather than doing the profitable tasks. You always need to be asking yourself what am I working on now?

Is this task moving me closer to my goals or away from my goals?

This is a tough questions because it is easy to say yeah. But you need to be brutality honest when you answer this question. The more honest you are with yourself the more you will achieve the goals you set. Is it clear and simple how you are moving towards your goal? Have you taken the time to define your goals?

This goal needs to wake you up scared but with the energy to make it a reality.

And let's face it. It is going to take 10 times more effort than you thought it would.

It's going to take 10 times more work that you thought it would.

There is always going to be something that is wanting your attention and asking you to settle for less than you want.

But I can promise you this. The one thing I didn't want to do when I was sitting on that couch in that cold Calgary apartment was this. I didn't want to have to go back to Australia and face my family and show I had failed to make it work.

I didn't want them to think I had given up. I didn't want to give up on myself. This was enough to cause the spark of action to happen.

Focus on mastering the basics and the rest will fall into place.

Creating cash flow is a simple art of controlling the leads.

This is one of those basics I didn't really understand. I thought other people would send me business.

I thought my products and services would sell themselves. But that is not true either.

"Outsource the marketing means you outsource the cash flow."

The sooner that you can understand that one of the most fundamental basics in your business is controlling your lead flow means you can control your sales.

Never outsource the marketing as your business lives and dies by it's marketing.

This is the lesson that I had to learn in the apartment in Calgary. I was hoping that my business partners would take control of the marketing and I just had to worry about the product. But this is not the case at all.

What I had done is outsourced the marketing which meant that I outsourced the cash flow. To allow someone else to tell me what and when I would be paid.

My entire focus with every business I am involved with now is that I control the marketing. That's one of the many reasons my core business now is QuizLabs.co where I help people take control of their lead generation.

We have even setup a 30 day challenge to teach people how to generate 101 leads within 30 days. Because this is what at the time I didn't know how to do. I relied on that hope marketing by attending event after event looking for someone to work with.

This is not an easy nor scalable way to generate business. Lead generation was the challenge I had in all my early ventures. I thought that this basic step would be handle if I just made the product better. But that is not the case at all.

Lead generation is one of those basics of business 101. You only need one simple marketing campaign that generates qualified leads and sales to create the wealth, happiness and freedom you desire.

Take the time to master this basic skill of generate leads and you will find your business choices become easier.

From every failure there is a lesson. It is only a failure if you did not learn the lesson you needed at the time. Understand that failing is going to be a part of your daily life and it's your goal to unlock the lessons within each failure.

Remember your awesome and have awesome to share with the world. It's your moral obligation to make a difference and leave this world better than you found it.

Share your awesome!

EVERYBODY HAS A COMING OUT STORY

DIANE CONKLIN

Growing up on a 75 acre farm, in rural Ohio, taught me a lot about life and business. Some of those lessons have served me well, in my almost 20 years in business, and some haven't fared as well. I'm grateful for all of it.

There are many traits that make you a success in life and in business. Here are a few that have served me well: discipline, hard-work, honesty, treating people the way you want to be treated, having a whatever-it-takes attitude, hustling, cooperation, completing tasks, and the list goes on.

The one thing that can, and will, hold you back more than anything else is what my dad called "the six inches between your ears." Today, people refer to it as your mindset. What you think about and how you think can catapult you to the top or keep you stuck. The good news is…you get to decide…and, you can always decide again! Tomorrow you can start again! Or you can start again in the next moment…it really is up to you!

Every person in the world had to overcome some things to reach their goals and to achieve what they define as success. Some have to overcome more than others.

I faced some adversity pretty early in my life, when my older brother was run over, and killed, by a school bus, in front of our home. He was six and I was three and a half. It's the first day of my childhood I vividly remember.

I lost a lot of people, family and friends, people I was close to and loved very much, before I was a teenager. Too many. Many more than most people I know.

I grew up playing sports, and I loved every minute of it. And, I was pretty good at it. Good enough to go to play NCAA fast pitch softball at a Division 1 school – at least before knee injuries and surgeries ended my career. I went on from there to be an award winning body builder and now own successful businesses and have my own not-for-profit foundation.

During all that time, I never felt like I completely fit anywhere. Somehow, I always felt a little different. And, I was never fully able to put my finger on it…

Until I turned 22 and realized I was gay (back then we were all just "gay." Today, if you're into all those labels, I'm called a "lesbian" – I call me "just me"!). This realization turned my world upside down as I struggled to deal with all that this meant to me.

This went against everything my parents, and the church, taught me growing up. And, it raised some pretty heavy questions for me. Was I going to be the "man" or the "woman" in the relationship? (I soon came to realize we were both still women.) What if people found out? Was I the only one? Was there something wrong with me? Was I going to go to hell because of this? Could I become straight? What about having kids?

So many things and the list is so much longer than the few things I've listed here.

As I navigated my life, my work life (at the job) soon became my business life and my then partner and I spent about 17 years running businesses together – and for the most part just being us, while "hiding" who we were (she was a career military office and this was before don't ask, don't tell). We weren't really fooling anybody but we weren't officially "out" either.

As we got more and more successful, Bill Glazer, who was then the President of Glazer-Kennedy Insider's Circle (GKIC), asked me to compete for their Marketer of the Year award. Since he thought it was a good idea, I submitted my entry and was honored to be one of the top three, out of 10,000 members at the time, to compete.

I presented my business, and the marketing I had done that year…and was voted, by 750 of my peers, who were in the room that day, GKIC Marketer of the Year!

I outed myself (as a lesbian) in front of the attendees of that GKIC event, those 750 business owners, many of them very conservative men and the world kept turning. I wasn't at all sure how to react to that knowledge.

A few months prior, I had started my own foundation because one of my passions is helping gay and lesbian youth who are being kicked out of their homes when they come out. (While my parents didn't formally disown me when I came out to them, nothing was ever the same again. I went from being daddy's little girl, his star athlete, who he spent time with and connected with through sports, to somebody he was unable to be alone in a room or a car with, for even a few minutes, in a matter of seconds when I told him I was a lesbian.)

When I finished my presentation that day, I had told 750 people in that room that 20% of the proceeds from all the sales we made were going to the foundation. At the time it was called the Gay Youth & Young Adult Foundation (it's now The Diane Conklin Foundation). And, I literally thought when I said the word gay from the platform that the ceiling of the hotel was going to fall in around me.

It didn't! Much to my surprise. And, the most amazing thing happened…people were coming up to me for the next two days telling me they thought they were the only one, or telling me how courageous they thought I was, asking how they could help, etc.

While I'd like to tell you I was completely out of the closet after that, I wasn't.

While I'd like to tell you I didn't lose any business because of my declaration that day, I can't. What I can tell you is I made a difference that day, and many days since then. I've touched people because I spoke the truth…my truth.

People are watching you. You are impacting people, whether you know it or not, whether you want to or not. Not by big gestures, or grand events, but by the little, everyday things you do. Just by being who you are you makes a big difference – a bigger difference than you may ever fully know.

Since that time, I've had hundreds of people tell me I've made a difference in their lives. After the break-up of my almost 20 year relationship (she was also my business partner), that some of my peers watched me go through, and come out the other side, stronger and better, many people reached out to me to tell me how much I inspired them.

Now, don't get me wrong, I still struggle sometimes – with a lot of things. And, I know this…I'm not a label. And neither are you. Your life and your business is what you make it. It's my choice, and it's yours.

In addition to the other marketing and business building stuff I do, I'm now stepping out to help other LGBT (Lesbian, Gay, Bisexual & Transgender) business owners grow their businesses with marketing and business strategy and leveraged implementation. There are more than 1.4 million LGBT business owners in the United States.

I'm also showing straight business owners who are interested in tapping into the $917 billion spending power of the LGBT consumer market how to attract and market to the LGBT consumer in the right ways, so they get clients for life and not just a one-time sale. Believe it or not, there are some very unique and different things to know about marketing to the LGBT consumer niche that are different than the typical marketing you might do.

This hasn't come easily or overnight as I've stopped and started more times than a 16 year old brand new driver learning to drive a 5 speed stick shift, but it's happening now and that's what matters.

What I've come to realize as I travel, and coach clients and teach and experience my journey is my story isn't unique. Everybody I know has something they have to overcome. Everyone has a closet they need to come out of. The reality is never as scary as what your head imagines it to be.

And, as my coach, mentor and friend, Matt Bacak, says money always follows the risk…with risk comes big rewards.

It doesn't matter who you are, what your past looks like, where you came from, who you love, the color of your skin, your gender, or anything else. Look around and you will find others who are like you who have done it and if even one other person has done something similar to what you want to do, you can do it too.

Finally, if you are gay, lesbian, bisexual, transgender or any of the other letters we add to our inclusive community, and you want to see an example of people like you who are successful and living in the world their way (all the way out, part way out, or in the closet) know that I'm here for you. I will support you in any way I can. All you have to do is reach out to me.

I'll never tell you I understand (because your journey and circumstances are different than mine) but I will always support you.

Making a difference while making a living…come join me…in Unity, Acceptance & Integration!

MY STORY

JOCELYN JONES

My Online Marketing Journey begins back in 2009. My husband, Jake was a loan officer and it was getting more and more difficult for him to do his job during that time. I was afraid that he might lose his job so I turned to the Internet trying to find something legitimate from home so that if he did, we'd have something to fall back on. I ended up getting scammed out of $12,000! Talk about a hard lesson to learn!!! Even though this happened to me…. I still had faith in Online Marketing. I picked myself up, brushed myself off and kept moving forward.

I struggled for years trying to figure out how to build a successful business. Along the way, I've had the opportunity to connect with wonderful people and have discovered that "Success Is A Journey, Not A Destination."

Making money online doesn't have to be difficult, once you know the "secret". Zig Ziglar says, "You can have everything in life you want if you will just help enough other people get what they want." Staying true to this principle, my passion has always been to help other people become successful with their business. It's not about me at all but what I can do to help them get connected to the resources and supports that they need.

I have always had the natural ability to connect with the right people. Everything really started to change for me when I had the opportunity to become Co-Owner and Director of Public Relations for the Academy of Home Business. My Business Partners and I went to a live marketing event (Marketing Mayhem), in San Diego, California, hosted by JvZoo in March 2015. It was at this event where I met Amazing and Talented Marketers.

This is also where I was first introduced to Dave VanHoose and Speaking Empire. Dave is known to be the Speaker's Coach and as soon as I saw him presenting on stage, I felt a jolt of electricity shoot through me! I KNEW that was what I wanted to do! I wanted to be able to share my message and travel the world. I was a Soccer Mom from Small Town USA, who decided it was time to stop playing small and made a decision, in that moment, that my life's purpose was meant to do much more than what I was doing as a Caseworker for people with Developmental Disabilities. It was time to take a leap of faith and Step into My Greatness!

Tony Robbins says to find someone that is doing what you are doing and model what they do. Success leaves clues. If you do what they are doing, You too, will be successful. One of the secrets to success is to find a Mentor who has already blazed the trail and learn from them so that you can cut the learning curve in half. There is no need to spend years trying to figure out how to do things yourself when they have already done the hard work for you.

I have had the honor to find a few such mentors that have trained me to effectively speak on stage. They have taught me how to speak on just about any topic at a moment's notice. This training and mentoring led me to becoming a Subject Matter Expert on Instagram.

One of my Biggest Fears was Public Speaking. What better way to step out of my comfort zone than to become an International Speaker? Through my mentorship I have been given the opportunity to speak in incredible places such as the Social Media Summit in Freeport, Grand Bahama as well as Dubai, Bahrain, and Pakistan! How exciting it was to share the stage with some of the Industry's Legends!

One of my mentors recommended that I learn how to use Instagram for marketing as it is much easier to find stages on which to present when you are a Subject Matter Expert. So, I dove into learning the intricacies of Instagram. At first, I wasn't quite sure why anyone would want to use Instagram. My oldest daughter, was always posting selfies and doing quick videos. It truly just seemed like a social thing. Most people feel the same. As I immersed myself in the different training courses, I was pleasantly surprised at the POWER of Instagram!

If you do things correctly, it is very easy to Attract Followers to Build Your List and Convert them to Customers. Instagram is the perfect way to Increase Your Influence. When I discovered how to connect people to people, it just made sense to me. I Love showing people how to have Success Through Socializing.

My Business Partner and I have since created our new business, JR Marketing Partners where we continue our mission of showing people how to properly build their online presence, using conversational marketing and social media to connect and engage with their perfect audience to turn them into raving customers. There are certain processes that need to be followed in order to have success marketing online. We teach people the mechanics and provide them with what they need so that they can either do it themselves, work with us side by side or we offer complete done for you marketing services. You know what they say, "Focus on what you are good at and outsource the rest". It is such a blessing to be able to be of service and help other people to achieve success and live the life of their dreams!

Section 2:

Finding Hope

HOW TO BE LIMITLESS

DUSHKA ZAPATA

I was having coffee with a friend. She was telling me she was stuck. There was no way she could get a job. Not in her current condition.

To which I eloquently said "Huh?"

"Dushka" she said. "I'm three months pregnant."

"But, how on Earth would that stop you from getting a job? Go prepare, give the best interview you possibly can and see how far you can get."
A month later she had a job. She then got paid through maternity leave, after which she returned to work.

I catch myself thinking like her all the time, convinced that there is so much out there I can't do. Because, it wouldn't work. Because others have tried it. Because it seems crazy.

That's when I remind myself I'm limitless.
Am I saying limits don't exist? Am I telling you that forces such as gravity are only an illusion?
Of course not. What I'm saying is *there are so many things out there that limit you that it's doubly important for you to pay no heed to the ones that exist only in your mind.*

In your mind, be limitless.

Don't allow your own assumptions to stop you. The whole world is ready to do that for you.
Which reminds me of the comic strip Garfield. Jon, his owner, finds both Odie and Garfield high up on a tree. *"But Odie"* Jon says. *"Dogs can't climb trees"*.

To which Garfield says *"it's amazing what one can accomplish when one doesn't know what one can't do."*

CHANGE YOUR MINDSET
CHANGE YOUR LIFE

DEANNA GRAYLY

I am currently an online entrepreneur living life my way, successfully managing my diabetes and inspiring others that they too, can do the same. It wasn't always like this.

I was born into a large, loving Polish family with seven siblings. I learned very early that our culture revolves around family and food. My grandparents and aunties and uncles and cousins came to visit every Sunday. We had regular family visitors and huge meals. We would sit around a heaving table of food. There would be all kinds of meats cooked in rich, sweet sauces. Even the different types of slaws and salads were covered in rich salad dressings loaded with sugar. The desserts were sensational and sweet. All the women had to be excellent cooks if they were to stand a chance finding a husband.

While growing up, I was only allowed to leave the table when I left a clean plate. I was reminded of the less fortunate. This "reminder" guilted me into cleaning my plate... right down to the last crumb. I was rewarded with candy or cookies for good behaviour, getting good grades at school and just to stay quiet. When I became a teenager, I discovered that my metabolism was not as fast when I began to gain weight. As we all know, growing through our teenage years is not always an easy task. My brothers made it their *mission* to tease me about my weight gain, which only further reduced my self-esteem and confidence. Due to these experiences, I often felt very self-conscious about my increasing size.

At the age of 12, my mother thought it was time to teach me about "diet and weight management." Needless to say, as you can tell from my story, mother doesn't always know best as I had already GAINED the weight! Through the *new* diet, my mother encouraged me to learn about what I ate and I did manage to lose a significant amount of weight. However, it never seemed to be enough to boost my self-confidence.

The die was cast. The eating pattern I was taught, to eat until my plate was clean, from an early age through my teenage years, and continued into my early adulthood. I was on a constant rollercoaster of weight loss and gain. When I felt down, I ate. When I felt happy, I ate. When I was bored, I ate. This pattern continued into my early adulthood. During this time, because of the eating patterns I developed while I was growing up, coupled with my poor self-esteem, I was unable to see people for who they were.

I was married at the age of 23 and still trying to discover who I was and what my life purpose was to be. My husband was 16 years older than me. The age difference added extra stress which aggravated the emotional eating pattern. However, we persevered to make the marriage work, enduring many obstacles and hardships.

I decided to become adventurous and I invested in setting up a household textiles factory with my husband. We became quite successful at it. It was fun having a fancy car and spending my share of the profits.

After seven years of marriage I became a full time mother to three gorgeous children and my job changed to a housewife. Being a housewife meant I was totally dependent on my husband to give me money for weekly groceries and basic needs. It was hard getting used to no longer having my own money and it knocked my self-confidence further. I only felt better when I ate my favourite candies.

Eleven years later my husband became seriously ill and passed away within nine months of the initial diagnosis. That was the end of my world ... or so I thought. Shortly after that, his business partner took away the factory from me and I had no source of income.

The sudden change of circumstances forced me to start over again and discover who I was. At this point, my life had many changes, twists, and turns happening.

I was forced to sell the house and move to an area more suitable for the children to be closer to their friends. I soon after met a lovely man and entered a stable, loving relationship. I then took on a regular job. After my children left home, I felt the "empty nesters" effect happening to me.

A short time later, at the age of 52, my doctor had diagnosed me with type 2 diabetes. I was in total shock. How could this be? What did I do wrong? Why me? I was in complete denial. I went home and "celebrated" with a big candy bar and sat down in front of the TV. The next several years were a constant downward spiral. I had very little energy, suffered from lack of sleep, and was constantly thirsty.

Later on in life, the "yoyo pattern" had reared its ugly head once again. Diabetes finally took total control of my life. My weight had tipped the scales. I no longer recognized the person looking back at me in the mirror. I decided to go on a slimming diet drink program but my holistic therapist stopped me just in time. Lilias told me as a diabetic, that I must go on a slimming diet with food otherwise if I lost weight too fast my body would go into toxic shock and I could have a heart attack and die. I later told my daughter, a qualified dietician, who became very upset with me. She reminded me of a friend's husband who was also diagnosed with diabetes 2, who refused to listen to his doctor. He was in his forties when he passed and never even got to see his children get married. My daughter then told me that she was expecting her first child and it was my choice if I wanted to be around to hold my grandchild or not.

I knew right then and there that I would NOT ALLOW diabetes to *run my life*!

It was time I took control of my future and my health. I finally began to listen to my doctor, my holistic therapist, and my life coach to reclaim the life I dreamed of. I no longer live to eat. I eat to live. I am on a strict diet. I got rid of my car to make sure I take regular exercise and wear a Fitbit to help me stay on course. I am now a grandmother with a loving partner and my life is finally back on track.

My story shows a great example of how we are programmed from early childhood by the teachings of our culture; from our eating patterns, behaviours, career choices and so forth. I believe you always have a choice to decide who you want to be.

Remember, only YOU control your destiny through the decisions that you make.

So if you change your mindset like I did, then you can change your life!

STATUS QUO

EILEEN FORRESTAL

I don't know when it started, I didn't really notice I was in a 'status' …. a plateau … a state of 'business as usual' …. but it probably happened when I was 'appointed' to my role as Consultant Anesthetist …. I had arrived! This is what I had worked and studied so hard for all these years. This was it! Acknowledgement. Recognition. Reputation. Success. Money. Security. Authority. Yes!!! Status!! And very soon, almost imperceptibly, it became 'business as usual'. Eaten bread is soon forgotten. My job was to put people to sleep, safely, to keep them asleep and safe while the surgeon worked his skill to remove or repair the broken or damaged area, and then return them to the world when they were now 'better'.

"You are … just …. drifting… off… to …sleep… now 10… 9… 8…. 7…. 6……….. Hello,….. It's time to Wake Up……

And in between … those hours of oblivion ….. while the brutality of surgery was being inflicted by the sharpest of knives with the greatest of skill on the most delicate of tissues …and all put back together with the tiniest of stitches, the ugliest of scars now hidden by the neatest of clean white dressings.

That was my job. The relief of suffering. Ensuring no awareness. Relieving pain with powerful drugs; providing numbness with epidurals and nerve blocks. Ordinary life in the Operating Theatre, the Intensive Care Unit, the Accident and Emergency Department, the Labour Ward …. Oblivion, Pain relief, Sedation, Resuscitation …. Birth and death and all of the suffering of humanity in between. My 'status Quo' – This is what life is like.

Every year, more my patients got bigger, with more complex chronic diseases, on more medications, coming with more pain … looking for relief, a cure, to be fixed, mended, made better …..

And I worked away …. Busily, silently, anonymously, hidden behind a face-mask, in non-descript scrubs … under increasing pressure, …. in a chronically underfunded health service trying to cope with an increasing burden of disease, almost breaking under the weight of unwell, unhappy, suffering people. No matter how hard I worked, I seemed to be swimming against the tide. It was exhausting.

Our newly refurbished operating tables could now hold patients weighing up to 450kg and we were attending regular training courses on Anesthesia and the Obese Patient. Status Quo? We were all asleep.

Call to Adventure

I agreed to accompany a friend on a fundraising 350km cycle in the Mekong Delta from Saigon in Vietnam to Angkor Wat in Cambodia. I agreed because I knew the Delta was flat as I wasn't so good cycling up hills. I had already climbed Kilimanjaro and trekked to Everest Base Camp a few years earlier so I was no stranger to rising to a challenge, but cycling through paddy fields in Spring appealed to me.

Fundraising however was not easy for me and I turned to my Irish Survivors Diary for inspiration. Flicking through the pages I had a brainwave – maybe the person who wrote the Diary would give me some of the proceeds of their Christmas sales towards my fundraising. Returning to the shop where I had purchased the diary I was directed to a village surprisingly nearby. Knocking on the authors' door, I was invited in …..

… to what transpired to be a new 'partnership' in a small publishing company, the only solution the challenge of keeping the diary alive. Delighted to be contributing to the survival of my beloved Irish Survivors Diary, and looking to the future with renewed energy and enthusiasm we changed the name to the Irish Get Up and Go Diary.

I completed my fundraising target, had a magical cycle through the Mekong Delta and returned to a whole new experience of getting our new fledgling publishing company up and going.

Challenges

I was now an Anesthetist with a small publishing business. This was definitely not the Status Quo. My colleagues were skeptical. My family were aghast. My mother worried – "what if they find out and you lose your job?"

I was loving creating the new diaries – they were filled with inspiration, motivation, encouragement, color, fun and life!! Every year we had an opportunity to include more great poems and stories and quotes. We started getting wonderful testimonials from our readers all around the world, most of whom had received a diary as a gift from a friend. This encouraged us that we were definitely on the right track. I wanted to do one for young people – "if only I had had something like this when I was growing up" people of every generation were chorusing. I found a brilliant illustrator and we were off, now we just needed more people to notice us. We started to approach the schools with a new homework journal. "No … we already have a journal" was the standard response. Except one. One was enough, for now.

And I had to learn about business, and financial planning, and profit margins … and I joined Women in business groups and applied for mentorships and attended workshops … And I had to learn how to deal with the interpersonal conflicts in our small fledgling partnership when we didn't always see eye to eye.

And then there was the guilt – I should be spending more time at Anesthetic conferences, not personal development workshops. I should be reading text books and Academic journals, not self help and inspirational autobiographies. What if there was a misadventure at work and I was criticized for not having studied enough?

This was my biggest fear, the one that kept me awake at night….

For 10 years I had a foot in two boats trying to keep both afloat and myself upright…..

Something had to give.

Decision time.

A phone call out of the blue invited me to a month long business women's retreat on Bali. Of course I couldn't go. Bali was on the other side of the world. I had work commitments, an on call schedule and it cost a lot of money. I didn't have enough holiday leave. No, it definitely wasn't possible.

I realized I had become trapped in a new, even more stressful, status Quo.

I took a month's unpaid leave and flew to Bali to figure out what I wanted to do with my life.

Discovery

I had never done a 'Profiling System' on myself. I had heard of Myers Briggs but that was all. I went into Medicine because I had the academic qualifications and I thought it was a safe place to hide for a shy girl with a speech impediment. Prior to my departure for Bali I was asked to do a Profile Test. Of the 8 Wealth Dynamics Profiles I discovered I was a Star Profile with Dynamo energy. Now this seemed to explain everything. Of course. That's why I loved working with the Diaries bringing those great, inspiring and timeless words of wisdom alive for a new generation. That's why I was never fulfilled hidden and silent in the sleeping world of Anesthesia. It was time to wake up. My 'purpose' as a star was to 'shine my light'. I now had to choose. I was ready. 'The cave you fear to enter holds the treasure you seek'.

I returned home with the news that I was taking early 'retirement' from the Health Service and would now engage fully with Get Up and Go Publications Ltd.

New normal

I could now risk speaking up at work without fear of censure or criticism. I was outspoken about the fact that the human body 'does not work' at 450kg. I was outspoken about the hypocrisy around alcohol in Ireland. I was outspoken around how irresponsible we are in our speaking in the listening of children. I could risk shining a light into those dark corners where people are 'suffering', - as "powerless victims of their circumstances" comfort eating, turning to alcohol, drugs, sex and violence to numb the pain; - with the intention of inspiring, educating, encouraging and empowering them to risk 'waking up' to the truth of who they really are – lovable human beings, whole, complete and perfect, a unique gift, deserving of compassion and the best life has to offer, so they can be fully alive in the world.

I could now shine my light wherever I went … I discovered my smile, which connects me with people everywhere – my words are words of truth and encouragement – I live a life of freedom, self-expression and power, happy and willing to contribute and make the difference I want to make in the world.

I am no longer the embarrassed, stuttering child, humiliated by the shame of her weakness – who vowed in a moment of anger and frustration – "you can shoot me, you can jail me, but you cannot make me speak", thinking I would be 'safe' in my self-imposed silence. Yes, I had survived, trapped in a 'sentence' of my own 'uttering '. Thankfully I was 'saved' by my own voice, by my own willingness to free myself from my own prison. I was 43.

I am now my grandfather's granddaughter, sharing his desire for peace and freedom. He used his life for the freedom of his country. I am now using my voice for peace and freedom in every human heart. Suffering, I believe, is optional. Hello. It's time to wake up.

ARE YOU LIVING IN A BOX???

JILL NIEMAN-PICERNO

As I sit here and look over the past 52 years, I wonder what I would share with myself if I were to go back in time, and had the opportunity to sit down with my 22 year-old self over a cup of hot coco? Wisdom …

Very simply put … I'd tell my younger self, to tune into your inner wisdom, trust yourself and live your life accordingly, in the present moment. Set your intentions and keep moving forward, ever so slightly, daily, consistently to become fully empowered. This is a simple, yet difficult concept to master.

We tend to put ourselves in a box. So, let's imagine, our box is approximately 20 feet long, by 10 feet wide, by 10 feet tall, with a steel lid on the top and a concrete floor. Imagine the walls are made of steel bars, about 12 inches apart, with each one of these bars represent a constraint. We are being constricted. Many of these constraints have been imposed by others, but many have been created by ourselves. Imagine further, that our egos are the ball and chain attached to our ankles with a steel strap. Unfortunately, when we live "Inside the Box", we are not going to be able to live the extraordinary life that we desire.

Where did all these constraints come from? When we are first born, we have to depend on others for everything to survive. Our parents, doing the best they can, normally pass along their individual internal constraints while parenting us. We are all creatures of habit, so many constraints have been passed down generation after generation. Then as we started to grow up and try to assert our inner wisdom, we were told, "**no!**" thousands of times, depending on how independent we tried to be. We were taught, during these formative years, how to depend on others for practically everything and conform to what is expected. We were taught not to listen to our inner wisdom. We were taught not to trust ourselves.

When we began going to school, more constraints were being placed upon us again. The schools pretended they were teaching us skills that would help us in our lives, but really we were all being taught how to think, feel, act and obey, to fit into the societal norms. We learned to give up our power.

Then, as school ended, we moved out of our parents' home and thought: Wow!… now I can finally live my own life, the way I have always wanted to. However, we now have to take care of ourselves financially. Most of us then get a job and are bombarded with even more and more constraints. The boss tells us when to go to work, when to eat lunch, when to take a break, how many hours we have to work, and even if we can take time off to do anything for ourselves or our family. Plus, while working for others, many of us learn to play small. We don't want to rock the boat or make others feel uncomfortable. However, what they do not realize is that the invisible energy of their internal thoughts, actually do affect others. It is as if they actually spoke those thoughts out loud. These actions just add more and more steel bars to the box.

Then a favorite pastime, of a huge majority of people, is watching hours and hours of television. While they are being entertained, they are fed a ton of information that constricts their free thinking thoughts. They don't even see that this is taking place and their box continues to wall up around them even more.

The sad thing is, that most of us do not even realize what is happening to us during all these years. We tend to just go along with the flow and learn to fit in. We live our lives on autopilot and think from our heads, abandoning our inner wisdom and truth from our hearts. However, this is not our fault. We didn't know any better, until now.

We all do have choices and can choose and manifest our own paths and journey. Plus, if we decide we don't like where we are going, we can change them. We should embrace ourselves for who we truly are on the inside, from our inner wisdom and manifest our fully empowered lives. It may be hard to break free from all the constraints of our steel bars from within our box, but this can be done and should be done sooner, rather than later. Our time is our most precious asset and shouldn't be wasted.

During my life's journey, I bought into the constraints of other people's thoughts, as some of my own, and ended up going to school, going to college, getting a good job, getting married and having children. I believed this is what I was supposed to do and my life would turn out to be … Happily Ever After.

However, after working in the corporate world for years, getting married, having children, moving several times and then having my marriage unravel, I had to take a long hard look at my life. I had not been living from my inner wisdom, trusting myself or living in the present moment. Yes, there were moments I was, but they weren't consistent enough. For the most part, I was living someone else's life. I was on autopilot, doing what I thought I was supposed to do. I was living in the box that others, as well as myself, had created for me. I wanted the freedom to live my own journey, even if it meant failing forward, as failure is just part of the process.

Over the next several years, I tried to manifest what I truly desired my life to look like. I knew I did not want to go back into the corporate world, as my two girls were young and I loved being a Stay-At-Home-Mom. My girls mean the world to me! So, I started researching types of businesses where you could be your own boss, so I could have the flexibility to spend time with and raise my girls. I always had an interest in Real Estate, so after much research, I became a mobile home park owner. This was an amazing business, where I learned a ton, but was not personally fulfilling. I had to do everything all by myself, which got pretty lonely. There was no relief from making all those business decisions, as I was the one wearing all the hats. I'm a people person, love being a team player and a big passion of mine is helping others succeed in life. So, I realized I needed another change and I started looking for my next journey.

Fortunately, during this time, I was exposed to Network Marketing and found what I was truly looking for. I would still have the time freedom to be a Stay-At-Home-Mom, while making a living and helping others succeed in life. Therefore, I sold my mobile home parks and aligned myself with a very successful mentor in the Network Marketing Industry. Aligning yourself with a mentor, coach or mastermind is very beneficial. I have used many mentors and coaches along my journey, plus have aligned myself with various amazing masterminds, like TPC. Through TPC, I have learned an enormous amount and there are a couple of the things that stand out for me that are very important to one's business success. They taught me to: Brand Yourself, not the company you represent and that Your Email List is Gold. So, definitely, use mentors, coaches and masterminds as they will save you a lot of time, money and energy. They have been through many of the obstacles you will encounter while moving forward on your journey and being truly open to learning from them will be essential to your life's success.

I was so excited to learn that the Network Marketing industry has "built in" mentors and coaches and the industry can be thought of as a personal development company in disguise. So, even though there are some people who do achieve the top financial ranks within their network marketing company, those who don't, also have an abundance of benefits. You will want to choose a company that aligns with your hearts intentions, where you can manifest your dreams. I truly love this industry so much, I actually co-created a song called "Livin the Dream" about Network Marketing. You will have the freedom of being in business for yourself, but you are definitely not in business by yourself. Plus, you can create your own schedule, while getting paid what your worth, with an endless earning potential. You won't have a boss, employees or overhead and can work from the comfort of your phone. So, you can work from anywhere at any time, in any time zone you desire. It's a blast hanging out with and traveling with positive, upbeat people. Network Marketers are fun people, who love helping others, are smart and have an inner drive to contribute to this world. One of the most wonderful benefits are the amazing, heartfelt friendships created within this industry. Thankfully, it doesn't attract negative, unhappy people and it's an equal opportunity for anyone. Then add in the tax incentives of having your own business and the flexibility of leaving an income stream as your legacy for your family are incredible! It's an eye to eye, belly to belly, heart to heart business, where you can live from your inner wisdom, trust yourself and live your life accordingly, in the present moment, being fully empowered. You are definitely "Out of the Box" in Network Marketing.

So, why would anyone want to live an ordinary life with all those constraints, when they can live an extraordinary life with endless possibilities? Only you know you, your inner wisdom, your truth and the life you desire. Imagine holding a TV remote control in your hands and clicking the button, running through the channels. Every channel you land on is a picture of what your life could be. So let's begin with your end in mind. You click to the next channel and there you are at the end of your life. Are you with family, friends, alone? Are you replaying all the extraordinary moments you have had over your lifetime or are you wishing you had lived your life differently? Whose life did you actually live? Were you on autopilot throughout it? Are you Happy, Sad, Content or Filled with Regrets? Only you can decide and unfortunately there are no retakes … So, when your heart monitor starts to beep for the last time, how will you feel as your life ends? Beep, Beep, Beeeeeeeep …

BEING TESTED TWICE

PAUL J KELLY

I am still grateful to have overcome a life threatening accident in 1997. An accident where I was dragged backwards by the shoulder, with the large back wheel of a 4 wheel drive tractor. The driver was reversing when suddenly he changed direction causing my body to be flung towards the tyre grip. It grabbed my complete body and folded me in two and squeezed me through a 400mm gap to the ground and my back snapped in two. An ambulance immediately rushed me to hospital on a spinal board.

After several checks and a cat scan, they found internal bleeding and said they did not have the resources to help me at that particular hospital. That was Saturday, 13th September and that day will never be forgotten for as long as I live.

I had to wait until Monday to get a bed in the Belfast City Hospital. Thankfully, with the surgeon's expertise, he plated and screwed me together again. I was then sent off to the Ulster hospital for a plaster cast.

All I can say is that I looked like a Teletubby. They sent me back to the Belfast City hospital, where I spent for a month lying looking at the wee dots in the perforated ceiling. The physio and bed baths continued on a daily basis. I found ways to keep my spirits up until I could finally walk again.

One way of doing this was drawing out the design for my own garage/workshop. I lived in an upstairs flat so the hospital couldn't discharge me until I could manage the stairs. Finding determination, I practiced on a flight of stairs at the hospital until I had no energy left

The nurses were not impressed by this but eventually I was able to go home. I spent the next year making very little movement. I returned to Belfast City hospital again to get the spinal plates removed. As you can imagine, I had so much discomfort for years which meant I was taking pain killers, patches and morphine injections. Even with Physio, I was still struggling to get back to normal.

Fifteen years later, I came across a product from Utah which was recommended by a friend that I met on a pain management course. I didn't have any questions about the redox signaling product. I just started drinking 2oz every morning and evening.

After a month, I started taking 4oz twice a day and 3 more months passed by with some slight movement. Then weekly 1 could feel my movement improve and thankfully I didn't need any more painkillers or injections. It had seemed so impossible that I would ever sleep soundly at night with ease but now, for the first time since the accident, I felt there was finally light at the end of the tunnel.

All was going great for me until one day, when we were putting up a carport and I was securing the skylights. There were 3 sheets for this and I had to go up a ladder approximately 3 meters high.

The ladder slipped off the fence and I fell down between the rungs and hit the ground with a loud slap. The slap was that hard, it felt like my body was strangling me. I was so winded, when I spoke you would think I was using helium.

Remembering back to the first questions the ambulance men asked when I broke my back. They repeated them and asked if I move my feet? I could so I heaved a huge sigh of relief but they put me on the spinal board for another run to the hospital.

I had more x rays and again I was able to work my way back to achieving some little movements despite the tears and tension at home. A few weeks passed but I was still not in a great place mentally.

I decided to take myself for a drive in the car. I headed towards the town of Omagh but had with no destination in mind. I turned onto a road I had not been on before and drove another 5 miles. I saw a picnic site, just past a hump back bridge. I went a little further beyond it and then decided to turn back and park up.

I left the car and walked along the raging river's edge. There had been a massive downpour of torrential rain earlier on that Sunday evening. A local fisher man stopped and told me, "I've never seen this river so high in 20 years" and on he went.

The water was swelling up on the archway of the bridge and the strong current forked off in both directions. I climbed up on the wooden ledge for fishermen and threw my leg over the wire and I felt myself starting to shake. There I was gazing distraught at the rapids of the river, ready to jump in. Suddenly a voice inside me started repeating over and over "you have to be worth more than this, be fearless!"

Still shaking and feeling cold, I managed to climb down from that ledge and before I knew it, I was back at the car. I sat there for a while before I started the car and headed back towards the town of Omagh.

I was not in the best shape. Between floods on the road and now the floods coming out of my eyes, it was getting difficult to see to drive. I was approaching the Tyrone & Fermanagh hospital sign. Something was telling me to go in as I needed help. I drove the car into the high rise building but could not find the entrance, shaking door handles as I walked around the building.

Eventually a lady opened a door and it was like she knew I needed help. I was at the wrong wing of the hospital but thankfully she gave me directions to reception and still shaking I followed her instructions.

When I entered the building there was no staff to be seen, just in patients. I sat down trying to contain myself. A guy with scars on his wrists, arms and his face came over to talk to me. He was very curious to know who signed me in and how long for. He then proceeded to tell me all about the police arresting him and his overdoses.

An hour passed and still no staff but he had to go back to his cell for the night. All his stories calmed me down before I realised my mobile had been ringing and there were messages from my wife telling me to come home. She kept saying Jason is looking for you.

To this day, I believe and trust I am living the best life I can live and tomorrow has more to teach me than yesterday. I've been told many times by others I was kept here for a reason and I believe this as well.

Today I absolutely love helping others with all types of health challenges and seeing them gain full health again. I do this by explaining the importance of keeping your body alkalised because most people keep their bodies too acidic which invites in ill health.

BE READY TO DIE EVERY SINGLE DAY

HENRY GOLD

It is not a promise to others, spouse, parents, or family. Instead, it is a promise to you and you. The question you need to ask yourself is… "What do you tell yourself every single day?" When you say you are going to do something, do you actually put your heart and soul into it? My point is… "Are your words worthy for others to rely on?" or "Are your words are just another broken promise?"

You see, it is easy to stretch the truth on those things you are going to do versus actually get them accomplished. When you say you are going to lose your weight, are you really going to complete that task? When you say that you are going to complete a project, do you actually take the steps to get them done?

If not, how do you expect other people to rely on your words?

You see…

The majority of the human beings make one broken promise after another. They can't say "no" to certain requests even though they know in their heart that they can't get it done. In the end, they keep making promises they can't keep at all. In the end, people associate "broken promises" with their names.

The next question is… "How do you start keeping your promises?"

It is very simple, really. In fact, start keeping your words even though you have to go through pain and sleepless nights on accomplishing what most people called the "impossible" in life.

I had been overweight for the majority of my life. Last year, I reached the peak by weighing 238 lbs. As a guy who is only 5'7, it was a lot of weight to hold. In fact, I felt that my system started to break down. At one point, I've almost lost 90% vision on my left eye and 50% on my right. My doctor then told me that I had kidney, liver, and heart related problems. To make things worse, my relationship failed making me live a life in utter misery, to the extent of fearing that I was about to lay on my death bed sooner rather than later.

It was in that moment, I had to make a critical decision.

I could either easily blame the world on how things were unfair, prepare myself to be inside a casket and go six-feet under (or) take charge of my life. At the same time, I made a commitment and told myself that every word that came out from my mouth was my executive order. So, I created a list of the tasks I wanted to accomplish:

Get six-pack abs.

Serve my clients with my heart and soul.

Surround myself with individuals who share my goals.

Remove all "takers" and "narcissistic" people from my life.

At first, I had a lot of doubt. For many days, weeks, and months, I cried for my failing relationship, health, and regretting the fact that I surrounded myself with narcissistic people who took away my self-worth, integrity, and self-confidence.

However, as I stayed focus on my new vision in life, I constantly reminded myself that… "My words are my executive orders".

In less than a year, I've lost 60 lbs. and now have a four-pack, steadily heading towards getting a six-pack. I have had many successful clients who told me that they loved me for the transformation I have done in their life. Furthermore, I've had many friends who visited me from many different states and countries almost every single week. All of whom are "givers" and I cherish them dearly. And to top it off, I now have network with best-selling authors, CEO's of public companies, and serial entrepreneurs who have built seven, eight, nine-figures, and even a billionaire!

Where did it begin? It started from my very own words.

The question you need to ask yourself is… "Are your words your executive orders?"

If they're not, isn't it time for you to change that? Isn't it time for you to become a reliable person and become responsible for every word that comes from your mouth? If not now, when? If you don't believe and execute everything that you say, how do you expect others to trust you?

Again, everything starts from you. Everything starts now. There is no "fear". It is all about execution. In fact, whether you like it or not, 50 years from now, you are going to be six-feet under anyway. This includes all those hecklers, haters or narcissistic people that will not do anything to improve the quality of their life.

Why NOT be ready to die every single day? Why NOT push yourself forward where you give everything you got and die empty every single day?

Don't make excuses. You are the leader of your own life. You are the person who is in charge of your destiny. If you are not willing to lead your own life, how do you expect to have a fulfilling life? Again, everything starts from you. No excuses, no what if's, no buts. It is now or never. Period.

STAYING STRONG

ANI CATINO

This is the story of our family and our challenging times and my spiritual beliefs.
For confidentiality purposes, , I will not name my sons' real names.

Year 1965. The time, when there were no computers, no mobile phones, no technology.

In fact, TV showed just one channel or two and few households could afford them.

That was the year I was born. My mother was an ordinary housewife with no high expectations, my father on the other hand, was a well-educated businessman travelling the world and spoke seven languages. Sadly, he died when I and my sister were still young.

After his death our world was destroyed. but living with our grandparents was a big support for all of us, for them showing great affection to us.

A few years later, our mum remarried. As bad as the word "Stepfather" sounds, although strict, he was actually a very kind, loving, caring and a considerate man who took us under his wings and brought us up as his own. He always made sure we had a good education and taught us to have good manners, so we would be respectful members of society. Regardless his discipline, I spent my childhood very happily and enjoyed every minute of it.

During the time I was growing up, I had three accidents where I ended up in half-coma which I survived them all. I then believed that, the life would either have very happy or very sad events for me in store. I could only realize I was right many years later!

As the time flew by, we lost our grandparents within the few years of each other. Their loss left a huge emptiness in our lives. So, in my early twenties, particularly after my grandmother's death, I decided it was time for me to have a new adventure so I travelled to the United Kingdom with new beginnings. In time, I managed to study English and Italian and working at the same time where I met my husband. A couple of years later, we got married but we never knew our lives would change forever.

One year later, our first son Jason was born 7 weeks prematurely. Although, we were over the moon with his birth, he would have health problems. While in the special baby unit, and only five days old, he had to have a stomach surgery. Following the surgery, he was then diagnosed with Pulmonary Stenosis-a heart condition- that, the blood flow from the right ventricle to the pulmonary artery is obstructed.

Once Doctors diagnosed his condition, they decided to operate on him when he was older. He eventually had it done when he was four years old. That was around the time when our younger son, Tom was born. So, our emotions were all mixed with the happiness and sadness at the same time.

Luckily, Jason's heart operation went very well and soon after that he was discharged. When we took him home happily and thinking that the most difficult time of our lives was over. Tom was diagnosed with a similar heart condition, but more severe.

Three years passed by and our life was happier, until one day-Tom had a cardiac arrest at his follow-up appointment- where he was due to be seen by his cardiologist. I always called that day one of our luckiest day of our lives, as he survived coincidentally for being at the wright place at the wright time!

Once again, we had to face up another heart surgery, this time for Tom. After the surgery, he recovered as well as expected and stayed in the hospital for almost three weeks before he was discharged. By then, It was about the Christmas time. When everyone thought of Christmas parties and gifts, our only wish was having Tom home. Our wish came true. Having Tom home for Christmas after two cardiac arrests and a surgery was our Best Christmas Present Ever!

But I knew there was a reason for Tom to survive them, against all odds. He became one of the kindest, most helpful, considerate and the sweetest boy, any parents would be proud to have.

After a few adventurous and challenging years, I decided to study and work during Jason's and Tom's early years of their childhood. Leisure, Travel & Tourism has always been my desired field due to my outgoing and sociable personality. I then applied for the course which lasted two years along with the other qualifications. I knew, one had to study hard to get somewhere and the learning was a lifelong aim for my self-development. Although, my sons health problems continued and had regular hospital visits, I successfully completed my course with the Distinction which I was very proud of to have.

In the following years, I continued studying further, with an interpreting degree to do the work I now love doing. For the first time in years, since our sons were born and their early childhood, we were settled and things were looking good, as by then, I had a working life and the boys were happy and as healthy as they could be. We thought, it was time for a change and a fresh start, and wanted to leave the bad memories behind. Since, Jason was also graduating from his primary school, we made a decision to move to a different area where the schools were very good. We were so excited for the move and so sure we would be even happier.

However, I should have known this happiness wouldn't last!

When the boys started their new schools they seemed happy. Tom immediately settled his new school in 3rd grade and made friends quickly. For Jason, however, it was a different story. Although, his first two years in his high school were fine and he seemed ok-although not very happy-we thought it was due to his adolescence, so it was normal to have mood swings. His shyness since his primary school, was also part of his personality so we didn't make any fuss out of it. I wish we'd made a fuss then so we would have known he had Autism earlier!

Autism is a lifelong condition that, causes lack of social interactions, eye contact, speech problems, behavioural disorders, learning disability only the few symptoms of many. It can vary from, individual to individual. If not known or diagnosed and act accordingly, from a young age it can have a devastating impact on the individual's mental health.

There are many autistic people in our society, and in the world, whom are not aware having the condition and feel always awkward about themselves but can't explain or understand why. This is because autism can vary from mild to severe and some can have it so mildly that it can go without noticed for years. What we know though, if the autism is diagnosed from an early age there is more chance and likeliness to manage it and having as normal life as possible with guidance and appropriate education and school.

You see, I wish Jason was diagnosed when he was much younger, so that, it wouldn't be such an ordeal for any of us, particularly for him.

By the time he was in the 9th grade, he became more and more withdrawn, aggressive and wouldn't want to go to the school. We had several meetings at the school where he attended, to come with some strategies and solutions. But nothing worked. Although, he was seen by a few Mental Health Specialists, they never understood the reason of his unexplained behaviour, until finally one day-a psychiatrist suspected he might have had Autism- EUREKA! His answer made sense finally, so he was referred for more specialist tests to confirm it. He was then officially diagnosed with Autism at the age of 16, an age where young people should live the time of their lives, when Jason was hit by a bomb and had been in denial of this lifelong condition. But who could blame Him?

Unfortunately, the confirmation of his diagnosis of autism came too late as that was the same time when he had just graduated from his highs school. What made us more furious, we had no support, no guidance after his diagnosis. It was a huge straggle to cope with his behaviour regardless our efforts and kept asking for appropriate help from professionals, but nothing happened.

In the following years, we encouraged him to get a higher education and he did manage to study, but never seemed happy. After he became an adult he met with a social worker who managed to get him accepted into a supported living facility, after much discussion and effort with the services.

We thought his life would improve and he would be managed with the staff support.

How wrong we were!

It's been three years since his move, but his mental health continues to deteriorate, even though we always remind him of our love and support by taking him home regularly and doing family outings with him.

I love living in the UK, but one of the things that UK Government has to make improvement is Mental Health Services. Because, there is never enough support by specialists and always lack of the qualified staff like social workers or Psychiatrists.

As Tom, my younger son, he went through another heart surgery at the age of 19, after 15 years since his first one, yet he never complained as he is such a sensible guy for his age. What a difference!

People including the members of my family keep asking me how I can remain so strong and keep going. Actually if it wasn't for the events and experiences that I've had, I don't think I would be as strong as I am now.

My spirituality and my religious beliefs for being from a Catholic background, have also my strength. I am a great believer in God, therefore my faith helps me to manage with everything going on in life. When, there are difficult days and events, it is my prayers that get those times over.

Every child is different and individual, they all need love and care. However, if a child with living and caring environment is still not happy, there's definitely a hidden problem or a cause. So, do not ignore any unexplained behaviours, because sooner you know better for everyone.

So, here we are again, still looking ways of improving my son's life, especially his mental health and we won't stop until we find him the appropriate place for him, and until we get our -once happy- little boy back again.

So, we will have to fight for Jason and not give up.

SECTION 3:

GRATITUDE

THE IMPORTANCE OF HAVING THE RIGHT PARTNER IN YOUR LIFE

DAVID PERDEW

A few weeks ago, my wife Charlsa and I were sitting with a group of friends. These folks know us really well. Someone complimented us on what a great relationship we have.

I smiled with pride. Lots of pride. And being less than humble, I said, "You know, I was just thinking about that very thing not long ago. I really think Charlsa and I should do relationship workshops."

She was sitting across the table from me with a dumbfounded look on her face.

"David, how many marriages do we have between us?"

"Oh yeah," I said. "That would be five."

Everyone laughed and said that maybe they should do the opposite of what we do. Sure. Good luck with that. For sure, do the opposite of what we DID, but pay attention to what I'm going to tell you now.

With five marriages between us comes a lot of what-not-to-do-if-you-want-to-stay-married-really experience.

Charlsa and I both have been married twice before.

We had vowed (many years before we met) that we were done with long-term relationships. We had not planned to be involved in "real" relationships again. They were too difficult and we were obviously not very good at doing the marriage thing.

But 18 years ago, when I was 45 years old, I rolled up on my Harley to RJ's restaurant in Atlanta to meet this "fantastic woman." Our mutual friend who practically browbeat us into meeting said that I was an adult and needed to meet her especially since she was "more your age."

"Don't be concerned," she said. "She's amazing."

That's what concerned me.

I'd been putting off this blind date for 3 months. She *did* sound amazing, exactly like someone I could fall for easily. That's the last thing I wanted.

She was beautiful, 5 years younger than me, and an accomplished opera singer with the Atlanta Opera for 13 years. She was known as one of the finest vocal coaches in the Southeast. The Atlanta Opera Chorus Master sent lots of aspiring singers her way.

She didn't really fit my dating patterns over the previous 3 years. I'd been dating 25 year-olds for 3 years with absolutely no intention of ever getting married again. And when someone made the mistake of saying…you know, we should really take our relationship to the next level…well, all you could hear from me was the door slamming shut.

I was gone.

But it was the spring of 1998, and an incredible day for a ride on the motorcycle.

Of course, since that was my only mode of transportation and had been for nearly 3 years, every day was a great day on the bike. That bike was my declaration of independence. It was the barrier that shielded me from anything that invaded my space.

After roaring up to RJ's and parking conspicuously on the sidewalk, I walked in, spotted the only woman sitting alone and pulling out the chair to sit, I said, "You must be Charlsa."

"And you're David?"

"Uh-huh," I said. She certainly was beautiful with her penetrating eyes and jet black hair. I also noticed she was wearing huge, funky Frankenstein-type boots that seemed way too big for her little body, but awfully cool.

I'd been dreading this blind date. It was my first – ever.

"So, what's your story?" she blurted out.

This was NOT her first blind date, obviously.

Before I could answer, she said, "What kind of bike is that?" pointing to the motorcycle sitting on the sidewalk in front of the café.

"Harley."

"What kind of Harley?"

I cocked my head. "Dyna."

"What kind of Dyna?"

Curious now, I said, "Convertible – what do you know about motorcycles?"

"I've got a Honda Nighthawk," she said.

Crap, I thought to myself. *This is going to be serious.*

And it was. It was fast. We were married 6 months later. Six months later, we got her a Harley too because she was tired of riding on the back of mine.

We loved hanging out with one another, but we were as different as night and day in many ways. I was an entrepreneur and moved fast with the idea du jour. I was also willing to bet the farm on that idea, often without really thinking it through.

She was a hip, socially liberal beauty, but a fiscally conservative teacher with a good retirement plan who focused on pragmatic security foremost.

But we had a spiritual connection. Not really New Age-y, but certainly we both were interested in the New Thought movements, especially that of Ernest Holmes and *The Science of Mind* philosophy that blossomed and grew from the 1920s.

And we both were on a quest to live a life of high integrity, and to be impeccable with our word, the first of *The Four Agreements* as authored by Don Miguel Ruiz. We found ourselves having deep conversations and sharing our secrets quickly.

Then, the boundaries were established.

I could be a hothead (probably the reason for the 2 previous marriages), and a little passive-aggressive sometimes (maybe a lot).

A couple of months after we married, I said something a little louder and a little more aggressively than she was used to.

She slammed the back door, walked to the middle of the back yard and stood for a moment.

Here we go. This is the way it starts, I said to myself. *Say something stupid, and they leave.*

Then, she turned and walked back into the kitchen where I stood looking out the window.

"This can't happen," she said. "If this relationship is going to work, you can't scare me. And I can't run. That's a deal breaker."

She was setting boundaries and delivering consequences, yet committing to work through differences. That was new, and it got my attention.

What an "adult" thing to do! We actually talked about something that bothered us. You have no idea how hard that is for me. Even today.

But we both committed to doing that.

As I dug into our relationship, I found more differences.

She's not a movie-goer. I'm a fanatic. She goes to bed early. Early for me is midnight. She's a vegetarian. I'm a wannabe, but love a good burger. She's a health fanatic that never misses her morning run. I'm a wannabe who would rather put it off until it's too late.

Yet, we love each other. We're best friends. We support one another in good and bad times. And we want the best for the other. Always.

We have a lot of boundaries.

If either person cheats on the other, it's over. There is no *let's-work-it-out-we're-only-human* excuses. We believe in forgiveness, but responsibility too. An affair, which we'd both been victims of, would be an incredible betrayal of the trust and respect we have for one another.

So we made a rule.

If either of us breaks other personal commitments, there are dire consequences too. We keep a list of those things that are really important to us.

On everything else, we compromise.

And we communicate. When we don't, we have trouble.

In the book, *Emergenetics: Tap into the New Science of Success*, four types of personalities are described:

- **Blue** - an *analytical* person who evaluates everything for value.
- **Green** – is highly *structured*, and always prepared.
- **Yellow** – scopes out the big picture quickly with a *conceptual* mind.
- **Red** – always wants to be *social* and to share everything.

Charlsa's green and I'm yellow.

Once we understood each other's styles and innate personality types, we were able to play with it a bit more.

I share ideas quite a bit, always cranking out new dreams and envisioning new adventures. Some become reality. Others are a pipe dream.

Charlsa, being the more structured of us, believed an idea spoken meant there was a plan in place. She began preparing.

I'm a yellow and she's a green. After we discovered the types in the book, she used it as shorthand. I'd spout off an idea or a dream and Charlsa, the GREEN, would say, "Are you speaking from the YELLOW now?" We'd laugh and move on. When an idea turned into a project, I announced it was now GREEN.

Red, green, yellow, blue, magenta, tope. Who cares?

Sure, it's a silly construct…but it's a framework for communication. Knowing how to communicate is half the battle to being able to communicate.

Because we know what makes the other tick, we're able factor that into our communication style.

And we value the other's opinion.

Charlsa is my partner and confidante. When I make good decisions for my business, it's because I've talked it over with her, and she brings her pragmatism to calm my overly enthusiastic reckless tendencies.

When she is feeling anxious because of family or business stuff that stretches her limits, she talks to me for comfort and to get perspective.

We're not really whole without the other.

So what have I learned by being married to the love of my life for 18 years?

First, listening is more important than talking. And harder.

Ancient Chinese philosopher Lau Tzu is quoted saying, *"He who talks doesn't know. He who knows doesn't talk.* "Amen, brother.

Here's an example: A few months ago we brought in a partner to help us with a series of software launches. The first one killed it. We pounded through the rough spots and missed some deadlines, but the results were great.

Toward the end of the launch, I went to Charlsa and said, "We're going to form a new corporation and bring partner X into the deal. We'll split this thing and crush it over the next 18 months with these 10 launches we have scheduled."

"Hold on big boy," she said. "That may be a really good idea, but what's the rush? Let's do 2 or 3 launches and decide then." I was crushed. I really wanted to move forward, but I knew if I did, I didn't have her support. That's important.

The second launch was so-so. Partner X's flaws showed up and they looked a lot like mine. We don't need two of me in a relationship, especially a business relationship. One is plenty.

The third launch was a disaster. Partner X saw the writing on the wall and dropped out of the future gigs. Whew! Glad I listened to her.

Now, she is not involved in the business on a daily business, but she knows me better than anyone. And she knows people. And she has years of being practical under her belt. Thank God. Being in a committed relationship is not always easy.

My dad told me long ago, "Marriage is an 80/20 partnership. And both give 80."

I admit that I had no idea what he was talking about when he told me that, and I had no clue why he was sharing this tidbit with me.

Plus, it couldn't possibly be true because it doesn't add up. An 80/80 relationship seems like a recipe for getting nothing done. The fact that he and my mother are the most loving couple I've ever seen even after 66 years of marriage, well, that didn't really register.

Many years later, 3 marriages and dozens of "relationships" and I now understand. I've finally got an 80/80 relationship. And I wouldn't trade it for anything. Ever. But if this doesn't ring true for you, I'm sorry. If you have a great marriage, you get it. In fact, you're living it. Once you see how this works, it's impossible not to. Both parties give 80 percent. This is the only way to maintain a fantastic relationship that grows daily. I wish it for you. Go make it happen.

ENTREPRENEURIAL LESSONS FROM MY EVERYDAY HERO

DAVID ASARNOW

When asked to share a story for the book 'Everyday Heroes', I had to think all the way back to my first job out of college. This time period was 15 years before I stepped out to become an Entrepreneur. The core of my story is the foundation that helped establish and frame me into the person I am today.

Ring, ring, rrrring... As I reached for the phone, I looked at the clock – 6 AM! Who would call me this early? "Hello?" I answered.

"David?" A strong voice with a heavy Lithuanian accent asked. "Did I wake you up?"

"Mr. Friedman, good morning! No, you didn't wake me up," I answered cheerfully, always acting as if I had been awake already. "How may I help you?"

(Mr. Henry Friedman was the head buyer of a large distribution company and one of my biggest clients. He was the first client I was managing as a 22-year old in my first sales job out of college.)

"David," he said, "we are out of foam plates and cutlery, and I need you to get a case to me before we open at 9 am."

"Absolutely, Mr. Friedman. You can count on me," I answered with a smile.

I rolled out of bed, jumped in the shower, threw on a suit, and hopped in my car. It was an hour drive to the warehouse from my apartment and then an hour back to Mr. Friedman's warehouse. After getting these frantic calls several months in a row, it didn't surprise me that the last sales rep, who had been with the company for over 25 years, was fired because he could not manage Mr. Friedman.

One warm Thursday afternoon in July, my sales manager John Jones called me into his office. I was still new with the company and providing excellent service to make our client happy, so I wondered what this talk was going to be about. "David, stop wasting your time with Mr. Friedman," he told me. "I know Henry is not easy to handle, and even though he is an important client you'll have to focus your efforts elsewhere or you are never going to grow your business. Mr. Henry Friedman is wasting your valuable time and our companies time using you as his personal errand boy." As I left John's office I was still contemplating how to solve the dilemma of satisfying my manager and my "challenging" client when Mr. Friedman called me. He said, "David, I want to meet with you this afternoon."

I'll never forget that day – the day that left an indelible mark on my thinking and actions and forever created an imprint that helped forge who I am today.

I walked into his office and took a seat. Mr. Friedman sat behind his big colonial desk. It was a cloudy day, which made the room look dark and gloomy. I wasn't sure what to expect. Was he going place a big order that I had been working so hard to secure?

Or was he going to tell me that since I had been his 'personal errand boy' for six months, he was going to "test" me for another six months? With Mr. Friedman anything was possible.

He said something to me in Yiddish, an old eastern European language. I was silent for a few moments and then politely asked, "What does that mean, Mr. Friedman?"

"Go ask your grandfather," he responded. "He speaks German. He'll understand and can translate for you."

I drove all this way for this, I asked myself. *To tell me a sentence I cannot even understand?* I sighed. For a brief moment I thought that John Jones could possibly be right. I should stop spending so much of my time trying to please Mr. Friedman. However, I called my grandfather, Papa Jules as Mr. Friedman asked me to do. I felt embarrassed and insulted when Papa Jules translated Mr. Friedman's words. Mr. Friedman had told me: "You don't think like a businessman!"

I was embarrassed in front of the person whose opinion about business meant the most to me – my grandfather! I thought of John Jones, my manager. He would tell me to "throw in the towel", after all he did not expect me to succeed. However, Papa Jules had a different insight. Insight that would shape the next 25 plus years.

"David," he said slowly to make sure I would not miss a single word of the wisdom he was about to share with me. "I understand you don't like what Mr. Friedman told you, and only you can choose how you are going to use those words. Are you going to run and prove John Jones right, or are you going to rise to the level Mr. Friedman is expecting from you, to take control and act like the true business professional I know that you are? You may feel that Mr. Friedman doesn't respect you, yet think about it, would he have shared that piece of information with you if he didn't expect amazing things from you?" Papa Jules was right!

This was my fork in the road. I had the opportunity to decide whether I was going to forge forward and become the best I can be and live up to my potential, or give up. Well, I was up for the challenge!

Have you ever felt so overwhelmed that you thought it would be far easier to retreat than to deal with the challenge? The desire to move away from stress (pain) is ingrained within the human DNA. However, what if you knew that within every stressful situation was an opportunity to create abundance, to transform this stress and overwhelm into something outstanding in your business and in your life? That is how it turned out for me.

Mr. Friedman was in his sixties and an immigrant from Transylvania. Mr. Friedman wanted the best service, to earn the respect that he had earned – and nothing less. Most people were not willing to deliver the level of service he demanded. Mr. Friedman wanted to know how committed a person was to him and his company before he was willing give you a real opportunity to let you grow. That is why he tested me like he did. Finally, after several months, I had earned his respect.

Mr. Friedman was a man of integrity and character, yet a superhero in the rough. Once I had learned how to polish him, he gave me all the opportunity to sell him my products. He shared with me that he survived the Holocaust. This was information very few people knew because most people could not sustain a relationship with him for any length of time. Mr. Friedman taught me this valuable lesson that I have taken with me and referred to ever since that day.

Relationships aren't assumed. They are earned. You have to be willing to do what it takes to build relationships that are meaningful. Many times this takes longer than you had thought. Persistence and determination are key factors in building relationships. If they are important enough to have as a client, you need take the time to build the relationship. When someone says *no*, take it as *'not yet'*. You may not have earned their respect or right to work with them yet.

The quality of your life (and business) is based upon the quality of your communication. Success in business is all about relationship building and connecting. People don't always say what they mean or know what they want. Asking powerful questions gives you the ability to connect and influence at a higher and deeper level, sometimes even instantly.

Feed your brain. Some people waste time in their car while driving or in downtime. Whenever Mr. Friedman asked me to drive 2 hours to and from the warehouse, I would listen to a motivational or business building audio.

Use the pressure and stress that you encounter every day to produce spectacular results for your business and life. Opportunities in life and in business do not just come along, they are right here with us all the time. We need to seek the opportunities, embrace them and then take direct, committed and consistent action to finalize the deal. When Mr. Friedman presented to me a major business turning point of opportunity the question was; Am I going to STEP UP and seize the opportunity? I did and grew my business with Mr. Friedman by 10x. Sales grew to over $2,000,000 over the next year and a half in his account alone.

Each of us encounters our own 'everyday hero's' all the time. The challenge we often face is appreciating the these heroes and the lessons and opportunities that they present to us.

How do we recognize these opportunities? How do we persist moving forward even though the obstacles seem insurmountable? We make a choice of what we want our life and business to be like and we embrace it and then create it. Appreciate all that you have. Realize that there are gems of wisdom and opportunity in everything.

Building something great takes time and it creates pressure. I know from experience that while pressure does not feel pleasant while experiencing it, emerging on the other side is an AMAZING experience and feeling!

How can you create your reality through understanding the natural phenomenon of human growth? Following is an example of two different people dealing with pressure. One person chooses to embrace the challenge and looks introspectively at what he can learn from it. This person grows and continues to persist even though it seems overwhelmingly difficult at the time. The other person gets angry at the universe, his boss, the government, his partner and the economy. He blames everyone but himself. Both people have experienced similar stressful situations, however one person grows tremendously and emerges happier, stronger and more successful, while the other remains in a state of blame, doom, gloom and disarray. What's the difference? Embracing the opportunity and all the pressures and stress that come with it.

You encounter "Everyday Hero's" daily through the course of life and business. Your ability to grow in your business and in life is dependent on your willingness to accept and embrace these heros and the opportunities and challenges they present. When you embrace these opportunities and do not give up, your mindset will change and it will allow and support your growth. When this happens to you, remind yourself that this may be a sign that you are building a bridge to cross the chasm for tremendous business and personal growth. You are almost there, take a deep breath, open your eyes and embrace the opportunity.

How did I embrace my first opportunity that Mr. Henry Friedman gave me? I choose to step up. Over the next 1.5 years I grew the business I did with Mr. Friedman by over $2,000,000 and my total business by $5,000,000 and became a top sales leader in the region and company every quarter. I embraced opportunity and created my own success from the challenges I did not originally understand. I was blessed to have my Grandfather in my corner as my first business mentor and coach.

I am eternally grateful for the opportunity to surround myself with a team of people who support me and help me realize the inner Hero I have within myself. Create a support team for yourself. Find a business coach or mentor that will help you uncover, create your own success stories. Have fun along the journey. Life's journey should not only be about reaching the outcome. It is about enjoying the journey along the way!

It is my passion to inspire entrepreneurs to believe in the dreams and goals for their businesses and to show them how they can truly reach them through advanced monetization strategies. If you want to monetize your business at a higher level lets connect! Visit me online at www.BusinessOxygen.net or www.HowToMonetize.net and visit the contact me page. I would love to hear your story.

MY PERSONAL STORY

LEE NAZAL

By all indications, it was a normal morning. I was delivering newspapers in a neighborhood about a mile away from my mother's house.

A man walking the street flagged me down, telling me that he didn't get his newspaper because I missed his house. The next words out of his mouth rocked me to my core.

"Get out of the car, or I'll shoot you!"

"What?" I asked, trembling with fear.

"Get out of the car or I'll shoot your ass!" he threatened, as he opened my door and grabbed my wrist. I complied, stumbling out of my car, trying to avoid altercation. He hopped in and drove away.

I stood there, shaken and paralyzed, as I watched my car leave me behind. Believe me, there is no feeling quite like watching a total stranger that's not wearing a valet jacket drive away with your car.

Why was I in this situation? What was I doing delivering newspapers at 25 years old that I would even be in a position to be carjacked?

In early 2001, my first son was months into his new life. I was in the subprime mortgage business, and every day at work crushed my soul. I left my job, virtually penniless, save for the unemployment checks.

Broke, with no other place to turn, we moved back home to my mother's basement. A low moment in my life, to be sure, relegated to charity at a time when my career should have started flourishing.

Without a job, we needed cash flow. The only employment I could find was delivering newspapers for The Washington Post. That meant I would need to get up at 3 AM every single morning, including weekends and holidays, to deliver papers for two hours a day. And so it was, on one fateful morning during my three year tenure as a paperboy that my life was threatened and my car was stolen.

While I was fortunate to escape the situation unharmed, the experience was an emphatic reminder of the state of my life. I had a young family, no money, barely a job, and a shattered confidence. My sense of self-worth was buried under hardened layers of doubt, despair, and hopelessness.

Being at rock bottom, there seemed no hope of escape.

Then I had a breakthrough that proved to be my saving grace.

My wife's aunt, Anne Conlan, offered to "work with me." At the time, I didn't know what that meant, nor what it entailed, but I needed all the help I could get. As it turned out, Aunt Anne is a Life Coach.

I went over to her office regularly. We talked; she asked questions; we talked some more. She saw something in me that I couldn't see. I was too mired in my own problems to realize what I had to offer the world. She helped me see it.

Since then, my life's trajectory has trended sharply upwards. In 2005, I founded a digital marketing agency. Not long after, it grew to become a tremendously successful enterprise. My client roster includes authors, attorneys, former pro athletes, and non-profit organizations, among others. For them, I generated millions of dollars in revenue to help grow their businesses.

With the success I've been able to achieve, I have the freedom to make a full-time living online and work from anywhere in the world. I also have the means, ability, and freedom to pursue my love of traveling. I've visited places all around the world, and I've embarked on incredible adventures. I've been skydiving in Fiji, paragliding in Switzerland, whitewater sledging in New Zealand, dog sledding in Alaska, and snorkeling in the Great Barrier Reef, to name but a few.

During one of these travels, something happened that touched my soul and would forever change my life. On our second trip to Fiji, we decided to visit an orphanage so we could teach our kids the value of giving and to show them a perspective of the world outside of our own.

We visited Treasure House, an orphanage that housed children and teenagers who were orphaned, abandoned, or abused. The rate of child abuse in Fiji has been increasing at an alarming rate over the past 5 years, and organizations such as Treasure House have become more important to society than ever before.

When we met the children, I did not expect what I found. Here are children who have encountered circumstances that no child deserves to face. And yet these children were happy, joyful, and full of life. It was due in large part to the care of the incredible people at Treasure House, who have dedicated their lives to changing the trajectory of these children and making sure they never have to feel that pain of neglect and abuse ever again.

I was truly moved. It was then that it occurred to me that the business I had built enabled us to have the freedom to travel to this corner of the world, and the opportunity to make a difference in these children's lives. My success has empowered me to contribute to this worthiest of causes. And while the children were beaming and grateful that a family from halfway around the world took the time to visit and play with them, it was I who was profoundly touched by their spirit.

Today, due to the trajectory-changing guidance I received, and inspired by the spirit and joy of the Fijian children, it is my commitment to do the same for other entrepreneurs. It is my mission to change the trajectory of adventure-loving entrepreneurs to have a real and lasting impact on the world by helping build and grow an empowering, extraordinary lifestyle business.

Whether you're trying to leave your job to pursue better opportunities for yourself and your family, or struggling to start the business you've been dreaming of, or desire to grow your existing business to unparalleled levels of success, I am dedicated to providing you with the guidance and expertise to break through your current limits, based on my decades of experience, expertise, and track record for results. In turn, it will empower you to change the trajectory of someone else's life.

So join me as we work together to impact every life and cause that's important to us. Because when you succeed, everybody benefits, whether it's your local soup kitchen down the street or an orphanage halfway around the world.

Let's you and I change the world together.

MY STORY

PAUL WAKEFIELD

"Once I discovered what I'm about to share with you, it changed my life forever…"

What I discovered has helped me through some of the toughest times of my life, financially, emotionally and personally. In fact, it inspired me to set-up my own business, it has allowed me to meet and work with some really inspirational people from around the world and I'm now in a position which allows me to share the very same information with you for FREE."

My names Paul Wakefield, I left school with no qualifications, I'm a failed dyslexic engineer and I didn't read a book until 2006 when I was 29 years old.

I was born on the 5th March 1977 in a town called High Wycombe, in Buckinghamshire, United Kingdom.

I have flashes of brilliance, lived a life of excuses, I've had massive failings, I spent 2 years sleeping on a sofa because I had no money, I've lost a house, fiancé, a business and I've spent 13 years battling to get access to see my daughter.

But it's not always been like that.

Let me give you a little background on myself: While at School between the age of 13 & 16 I had two jobs, I was selling programs at my local football club called Wycombe Wanderers earning £10.00 per match, I also had a paper round delivering a local Paper called the Star where I was delivering 750 papers on a Friday afternoon/evening and I was earning £55.00 a week. Within a few years I had saved enough money to buy my first car. That car cost me £2,500.

Sadly during my last few years of school, I was very heavily bullied by my so called 'friends'. Friends who I'd grown up with all my life. I can remember running home from school and being so scared of what might happen to me if I hang around. I use to come home from school and cry my eyes out because I was that scared.

I remember two occasions very clearly. One was on a Friday afternoon while I was out doing my paper round. One lad who had been bullying me for some time came after me with a gun. I'd never been so scared in my life. Luckily at this point in my life I was a very fast runner, I can remember running straight to a friend's house praying all the way that he was in so that I would be safe.

The other occasion was on a Thursday night after youth club. I was on my way home with a group of friends. I'm not sure how, but suddenly a message had got to me and my group of friends that these people were out and were coming to get me.

I kind of took this message with a pinch of salt and just carried on walking home. Within minutes, 7 people had found out where I was and again I found myself running for my life because they came after me with huge kitchen knives.

Now you may be thinking two things right now, one, that I'm a wimp for running away and two, why were these people bullying me. First of all, ask yourself this, if people were coming after you with knives and guns, wouldn't you run away?

Look, the truth is they were jealous of me. I come from a very small but very close family. My mum worked part-time as a cashier for a very well-known high street bank here in the UK for about 32 years and my dad was a factory worker, an upholsterer and a very good one at that. So you can see by this that both my parents had what I would call an 'average' job, certainly nothing that made my parents financially wealthy. Yet I was always looked at as mummy and daddy's little rich boy and that's what people didn't like.

When I left school I wanted to be a fashion designer, for whatever reason my career advisor told me to get into engineering so I tried my hand at being an engineer, after 3.5 years of hard work at College and working through my 5 year apprenticeship I was told I was dyslexic and to consider a new career…

I'd just wasted 3.5 years of my life doing something that I didn't want to do in the first place. I had only done it because my career advisor told me to try it. Let's face it these people are the so called 'experts' so of course I was going to listen to her.

The sad thing was I was now close to turning 20 years old. I was now out of work and had no idea what I was going to do or where my life was heading.

By now I was heavily involved with drugs. My life was a mess. March 5th 1998 was my 21st birthday, most people would be excited on this day in their life, but sadly I wasn't. You see, at 9am on my 21st birthday I was in a church at a funeral of whom at the time was my best friends dad. What's worse is that within the next 6 months I lost 5 other friends due to cancer and car accidents. I soon found myself having counselling. I was struggling to deal with life. My working career became a mess. I was in and out of jobs like a yoyo. I knew this had to stop but I didn't really know what I wanted to do.

After 4.5 years of counselling I had to sit back and have a serious think about what I wanted from life and where I was going. The answer I come up with was that … "I WANTED LOTS OF MONEY" … "I WANTED TO BE SOMEONE" … "I WANTED TO HAVE SUCCESS" … "I ENJOYED HELPING OTHERS" … "I WANTED TO GIVE BACK" and "I WANTED TO MAKE A DIFFERENCE IN THE WORLD" but what could I do that would give me all of this satisfaction. No one could tell me and I certainly didn't know. So I just carried on living the life I was living… which wasn't particularly good!

Allow me to fast forward…

In February 2007 I finally set up my very own business, it was Recruitment Agency specializing within the Automotive Industry. I thought I had cracked it, I thought this was the start of my dreams coming true and getting everything I had always wanted, but 14 months down the road I ended up closing this business, I had failed miserably and I ended up putting 3 people out of work. But I wasn't going to let this stop me.

In 2008 I took time to reflect on what I really wanted from life, how to use my skills and experience to help others. I made the decision to move on from a traditional corporate life and build my own home based business with the control, flexibility and lifestyle benefits that are really important to me. I had enough of intense commuting and exhausting business travel; I was no longer willing to make personal family sacrifices.

On October 26th, 2008, I started the business I have now. I was on crutches, sleeping on a sofa, I only had £2.87 in my bank, I had no customers, no Internet connection of my own, no website and an old Dell laptop. 7.30pm that evening I had arranged to do a joint venture with a guy called Tim. Thanks to this joint venture and a webinar that we did together, I made 128 sales of an eBook that I had written called The Difference Between Success and Failure and I made just over £6,000 in profit within 90 minutes. I felt like a millionaire! But then things very quickly went downhill again…

Four months after starting this business, between February 2009 and December 2009, my family and I had to deal with 7 family funerals. I lost my 4 grandparents, mums cousin and two family friends. This was the start of a 3 year battle with serious depression and social anxiety. Most days I never got dressed, I just sat behind my laptop pretending life was great. I was suffering really badly with a mental illness.

During this dark time in my life I decided to get professional help again from another councilor. It was the best thing I'd ever done.

I soon realized that all though life had been tough, I still had everything that I could ever dream of. I had things that a lot of people in this world could only dream of having. I started to look at life in a different way. I realized that only I could make things better. I learned gratitude. I stopped making excuses, and I went on to write a book.

October 2013 I was offered a publishing contract by UK book publishing company near London. Within two weeks of my book being published it was on sale in 24 different countries. My book was changing life's all around the world. I soon realized that I could use my story to help inspire and empower others to live a life of their dreams, but they had to stop making excuses.

I've now built a small global company, I've trained over 32,500 people from around the world, I've coached 100's of people, I've been featured in the book called The Laptop Millionaire, I spend 3 months of the year living in our family home in Goa and have an outsource center in Delhi with 90 employees.

My life has completely changed. My *"why"* is my family. I can now do what I want when I want and I spend my time with those I love.

My mission is to now create a safe and secure future for 600 children in India by 2030. Learning to be grateful for everything and everyone in my life changed my life forever. I also stopped blaming others, I took responsibility for my actions, I stopped making excuses, when I done this I became financially free… you can too!

My name's Paul Wakefield. I'm a failed, dyslexic engineer without a single qualification to my name. I've been bullied, I've been threatened, I've lost everything, but I kept on going. If I can do it, you can too.

Thank you for reading my story.

HOW GRATITUDE SAVED MY LIFE

DONNA KENNEDY

For as long as I can remember my mother asked that I be grateful for everything in my life. "Say your ten things" was my morning send-off as I left my house to go to school. Of course, as I did with most things then, I followed instruction – "I'm grateful for my new stickers, I'm grateful for my uniform, I'm grateful for my shoes, I'm grateful for my pet snail, Chrissy..." I just picked random things until I had ten. It was a normal part of my day. It was a habit, albeit a monotonous one at times. Little did I know that some years later that monotonous habit would save my life!

I will never forget the day my mother and I sat on my bed crying hopelessly in each other's' arms. I was fifteen, I was desperate and I was petrified, having just woken from a coma. A clock ticking on the locker next to my bed, my mind alert but my body like a lump of lead, part of me tempted to just let go and the other part of me desperately fighting to stay alive – it was the scariest thing I had ever experienced. And the worst bit was, it was self-inflicted.

I had intentionally starved my body and it had no choice but to surrender.

I was given one week to live.

From my mother...

"It was a mother's worst nightmare to watch her beautiful precious child suffering anorexia.

At first I didn't know she had the illness. I did notice that she wasn't eating very much but I thought it was a teenage phase. Donna was the fifth of seven children and at that time the fashion was sloppy jumpers and jeans, which hid a lot.

The first time it dawned on me that something was wrong was on a shopping trip to buy clothes. One of her sisters noticed how thin Donna was when she tried on clothing and she told me. The warning lights went on and I was vigilant from then on. I noticed how secretive she was around food, sometimes only eating a couple of apples for the whole day.

I brought Donna into the G.P. for a checkup and the doctor explained anorexia to me and how Donna felt she had no control in her life and this was her way of exercising some sort of control.

I talked to Donna and we tried to work out some sort of diet that she was comfortable with. She agreed to take a bowl of porridge in the morning and have a yogurt with her apples. It was a start. I tried to get her to eat but I had to watch very closely because if she got the chance she would go to the toilet and vomit.

Her weight went down to 31kg (5 stone or 68 lbs.), which is famine weight for a girl of 1.7 meters (5' 10") in height. Her pelvic bones stuck out and there was nothing but a layer of skin covering bone. She looked like a skeleton but all she could see when she looked in the mirror was fat.

I had some cameras that developed photos instantly and I took a photo of her pelvis and gave her the photo. I thought she might be able to see in the photo what she couldn't see in the mirror. When she saw the photo, she started to cry. She said she looked like a hippo.

It was so scary. Thinking about it now I can feel the sickening fear that was tearing my heart out of my chest. I felt so helpless and yet I could not give into that feeling. I prayed so hard every day for the strength to know what to do and for the patience and energy to keep going and to help my precious child to walk through the illness and gain her life.

I brought her into the G.P. again. Donna's blood pressure had gone dangerously low, her heart was failing, and she needed to go to hospital. After a week in hospital her weight had dropped by another 7 pounds, despite the best efforts of the hospital staff. My G.P. suggested that I stay with Donna during the days and try to get her to eat. She was almost dead. So, I got up every morning at 7am and made her a bowl of porridge and then her Dad drove me the twelve miles to the hospital. I stayed with her for the day until 8pm and I did this every day.

During the day I fed her and watched that she did not try to vomit under the sheets. I would read to her and a lot of the time she slept because she was so weak. But gradually Donna got better and we were able to bring her home. There was still a long way to go and I kept praying for strength, patience and understanding. One of the most difficult times was when she would literally want to disappear. Her bedroom at the time had a bed beside a wall and she would put her head and shoulders down between the bed and the wall and the most horrible moan would come out of her. My heart nearly broke hearing that sound. It illustrated exactly how she was feeling inside. For a mother to hear that sound from her precious child is not something that any human being should experience. I prayed for help and then I forcibly took her out of the "hole" that she had made between the wall and the bed. And I would lay her down to stop her trying to get back into the hole. Then I would just hold her. I loved her so much.

It took Donna a long time to get better. She had gone so low, having slipped into a coma at one point, but day by day we worked at getting her better – one step at a time.

When one is an alcoholic one speaks of the demon drink. It is very apt because with any addiction there is a demon attached to it. The demon anorexia lurks in the shadows waiting to gain control again. Doctors speak of anorexia as the way a person gets control in their life. But I know this to be flawed thinking. They do not get control. They lose control to anorexia behavior, which controls them, almost to death in Donna's case. The only way a person can have any control in life is to leave negative thoughts behind and never allow them into one's life again."

Looking back now, I can pin-point my moment of change and it wasn't when I agreed to eat or gain weight. Agreeing to eat was simply to stay alive, to keep the peace and go through the motions until I figured out how to not eat and not die at the same time. I continued to exist on a knife edge. The real change happened when I hit emotion hard, when I really felt the pain my family were feeling. The shock surrounding the coma gave me a literal wake up call. I knew something had to change.

If I wasn't to die, I couldn't live that way anymore. I had to find emotional strength somewhere.

That day I blubbered in my mother's arms, for what seemed like hours, not having any answers as to how to recover, other than the age-old "just eat" treatment. Gain-weight-and-you'll-be-fine, type thing. But I knew that even if I ate all day long I would eventually slip back. I needed something more if I was to get better long-term.

Holding me close against her chest like a baby, my mother cried "Donna, I don't know what to do but I prayed about it. Let's be grateful. Let's think of "ten things". What ten things can we be grateful for right now?" Grateful! What did I have to be grateful for? Was she out of her mind?

"Bear with me sweetie, please do what I ask.' She pleaded. 'We are at a place of desperation, a place where we have to do something good for you now. I don't have the answers but I have prayed and right now I want you to tell me ten things that you are grateful for. Just trust me. Let's write them down."

I was too weak to think, never mind write but as always, she stepped in when I needed her. She held the pen, ready.

Truly, I couldn't think of one thing to be grateful for in that moment. I had been living in a bubble of self-loathing and I couldn't see outside of it. I began to get frustrated and that frustration then turned to anger. I was so angry at her, I was angry at the world and I hated myself, but what choice did I have other than to trust her? With a very reluctant sigh, I agreed to give her logic a chance. I loved her so much and, even though I was angry, I trusted that there must be a valid reason for asking me to me to do this.

"I'll start you off. Look at your hands. Imagine life without your hands." with tears in her eyes, she searched for a glimmer of co-operation in mine.

'Okay that is one thing I could be grateful for, I suppose.' I was flippant in my response but agreed that I wouldn't like to lose my hands.'

She continued...'And what can you do with your hands? You're good at art aren't you?'

We sat on my bed for ages discussing what I could be grateful for. It took writing 39 things before I genuinely felt gratitude! I know that sounds selfish but I was selfish. I couldn't see past myself and starvation.

At first, I just didn't get what may mother was doing. But as we spoke, I began to understand. She too was searching for emotional strength within me and hoped we might find it in gratitude. And we did. I had genuinely forgotten how precious my life actually was, how precious I was. She was reminding me of the value of my life.

I have come to understand that gratitude is not something to be taken lightly. The day I became grateful was the day my life changed. I was gifted the foundation of gratitude, which has allowed me to become the empowered person I am today. Without gratitude life is just an empty existence. With gratitude, life can be lived.

To this day, I become consciously grateful every day for ten things in my life, just like I did when I was a young child. This is a daily reminder to choose life over death. We are here to live. Gratitude is the key to living life fully!

I DON'T CONSIDER MYSELF A HERO

DARYL HILL

I'm not sure why you should read this chapter because I don't consider myself a hero. The real heroes, in my eyes, are the ones who didn't come home.

I have this hang-up about drawing attention to myself. I feel more comfortable talking about the success of those I work with, because by doing so, it draws less attention to me. Those that I'm referring to, are the warriors in the arena, fighting the fight. I'm simply a guide that can help them on their journey home.

I have a tendency of serving myself last at meal time. It's just something that has always been with me growing up. It was further bred into me in the Marine Corp. A commander, during combat, or on US soil, always eats last after all the men in the platoon. I was a commander and there were many times I didn't get to eat a meal. You take care of your men under your command and you put their needs above your own. Just like a parent would sacrifice to make sure their children didn't go without. I have stood up many times in front of my Light Armored Recon Vehicle and told 250 marines that I was there to serve them and I consistently proved it to them every day.

There are actions and values from the Marine Corp that carry over into everyday life. How you respond to the experiences in the Corps determines how you might react to a similar situation in your future. You grow to behave the same, whether you are on a battlefield or on a baseball field.

Today I played basketball with a few Naval Academy professors, officers, and coaches. After the game, I walked out of the gym and ran into a very frazzled looking woman. I asked her if she needed any help. She explained she was worried about her son making it through the Naval Academy. She asked me if I had some insight and I gave her the most honest advice that I could. I said, "This place is about teaching leadership and values. Imagine your son as a ball of clay going into this academy and he will be molded over time into a statue of a soldier." She asked me to tell her the truth about how hard it is in the Naval Academy. I looked in to her eyes and said, "Every hour is a fight, and every day is a battle." She asked if it got any easier, I replied, "the only easy day here is yesterday," I spent four years being molded in the statue I am today. I had a tremendous amount of tough love and leadership lessons from the Naval Academy that made me the person I am today.

Life isn't all peaches & gravy and neither is life at the Naval Academy for a midshipman. There's a reason that every year 40,000 applications are submitted and only 1,000 new midshipmen are chosen. It's truly a special place that I was fortunate enough to have been accepted and then transformed into an honorable man.

My life wasn't easy before the Naval Academy either and I found many of my brothers had similar struggles when they were younger. When I was starting elementary school, I was labeled as "special" because I failed standard IQ tests. My mother didn't accept that label and had me further tested and discovered I had a form of dyslexia amongst other learning disabilities that today are my superpowers. I was very intelligent but my mind processed information differently than other children. My spatial recognition skills were very high and that is not considered on standard tests. If it wasn't for my mother, I would've never reached my full potential, and I would have lived with a label that would have limited me the rest of my life. Fortunately, at times, I tend to march to the beat of a different drum, and leave authority for other people.

My mom, who is one of my biggest heroes, worked tirelessly and sacrificed to put food on the table and she always made sure I had what I needed. She even hid having breast cancer from me because she didn't want to distract me from sports and making the honor roll while I was in high school.

I started receiving many football recruiting letters from colleges all over the country during my junior year. One day, I got an invitation to attend a Navy home game. I was at the kitchen table going through the mail and studying after football practice. Exhausted and sore, I tossed it aside without another thought and went to bed. As a single mom, she never missed anything even while working 7pm to 7am the whole time I was growing up. That meant we barely saw each other for 15 minutes before she ran off to work and I would be gone before she got home in the morning for school.

One Friday I came home excited because it was the only bye weekend in the football season and I had a whole weekend to go have fun with my friends. My mom came out of the kitchen with the Navy game invite letter in her hand and said, "Pack a bag, we are going to Annapolis, MD." "What?!" Obviously, my Mom knew the Naval Academy was a special place. And as usual, she knew what I needed, acted, and sacrificed her weekend off to get me there.

We lived in Jupiter, FL, so I wanted to go to the beach with my friends to surf and be a teenager for a weekend. After some moaning and groaning, I packed a bag and off we went. I didn't know anything about the Naval Academy so I had this preconceived notion that people were going to be a bunch of, for lack of a better phrase, geeks from the Geek Squad. Boy, was I wrong! From the second I stepped on the Yard (name for the whole campus used by the Midshipmen), I noticed they were anything but a bunch of people from the Geek Squad department at Best Buy. I remember going to meet Coach Runyon at the Naval Academy, he was the Wide Receiver's Navy Football coach recruiting me out of the state of Florida.

The weight room and all the facilities were state of art, and amazing. I got to meet a few of the players who had not dressed for the game and a few former players as well. We struck up a conversation and they shot straight with me. "This is a tough place and you have to truly choose and commit to be here." I chose the Naval Academy and made the commitment to become a Midshipman. Other than becoming a father, it was the best decision I ever made in my life.

Prior to the last football game against Army in the Ravens stadium before graduation, I stood in the locker room where many Navy Football Brothers had stood before me knowing the next fight after this one would be the real thing. This next commitment would be to my country and my brothers would be on the battlefield with me instead of the football field. And on this day Army our brother in arms would be our enemy. Often people ask me what it's like to play in the Army Navy game, and I simply reply, "you ever get into a fight with your brother?" Throw out the records and everything else you can measure because there is no measurement for the heart and discipline that goes into this game. Therefore, it's called the "America's Game." And as I did before every game, I looked at my brothers to the left and to the right of me and took the field with relentless abandonment for my body and made every hit count, knowing that today, after the final down, I would leave it all on the field for good.

Our coach and officer representatives would remind us that we were practicing for the real game that we would play one day, on the battlefield. They kicked our butts when we needed it and kept is in line when we were knuckleheads. Knowing that one day we would be leading Marines and Sailors on the seas and battlefields.

You see Navy plays its football games at Navy-Marine Corps Memorial Stadium in Annapolis, Maryland. The classic joke is of an opposing player or coach looking up at the stadium and reading the names of famous battles—Iwo Jima, Guadalcanal, Saipan, Bataan, Corregidor, etc. The player or coach comes away impressed, knowing that his team can never beat Navy. "Wow, Navy sure plays a tough schedule!"

Now imagine you are the coach of a college football team that is going to play Navy this weekend. You try to prepare a bunch of college kids that are about to walk onto the home turf/battlefield. That mental edge is exactly the mentality that helps Navy beat teams on the football field day in and day out.

On paper, an unranked Navy team verses #1 college team in the country, has the betting line losing by 3 touchdowns. The mental discipline and tenacity of the players, coaches, and the entire school is how Navy is able make teams like Ohio State, ranked #1 in the country, go into overtime. From the 2000 Navy team that I played on, we did go on to lose three brothers in battle. I would be remiss if I didn't mention that my teammates and I lost many more Naval Academy brothers that were not on the Navy football team, to conflict overseas and PTSD.

After the Naval Academy, I entered the toughest training for military officers in the Marine Corps known as the Infantry Officer Course (IOC). I was there with a bunch of men who stood for what they believed in. Now don't get me wrong we all had our moments of cracking jokes and making it through road marches which, sometimes led to 10 mile unexpected runs with combat loads, do to a code like fight club that is about all I'll say about the training, we had Marines who had left jobs that were there in New York City when the twin towers crumbed to the ground. There were also Marines who had left active service who came back in to serve even when they had no obligation to do so but because they chose to, these were the men I would soon cross the oceans with to protect each other on the left and right flank.

These are the true unsung heroes that never ask for the spotlight or look for it. They truly just see it as they doing their job and serving their country. And often in life, people emerge as heroes because they instinctively do things that ordinary people wouldn't choose to do out of self-preservation. 9/11 is a perfect example of this type of heroism. We watched firemen, policemen, and some civilians run in and out of burning buildings to save lives, without caring or knowing if they would live or die.

I was part of a battalion of Marines that lost 57 Marines to combat operations and since then many more have been lost to suicide than actual combat operations. You can read the book We Were One by Patrick O'Donnell to get a true account of what heroism is to a Marine. It's my mission to help those who are losing the fight of their life to PTSD. It's one thing to lose a brother in battle while you fight side by side for your country. But it's another thing to look down at your brother in a casket because he couldn't overcome the emotional and mental wounds caused by war.

I was fortunate enough to be spared and I actively got help for what is known as "survivors guilt" that weighed heavily on my mind and was starting to cause me severe depression. Why did they have to die and why was I spared? One day I sat down and talked to a Navy Seal who had dealt with that type of guilt. I told him, "I used to think I was fine because I'm home, and I'm alive with all my body parts, but the truth is I'm not fine." We had an unforgettable conversation that started to shift my mindset around what had happened to me by telling me his story and how he survived the a famous fight for his life that was national media and coming home how he discovered it after 20 years inside his own mind. His amazing story led me on a journey that I'm still on today.

He told me about Marine SSgt Retired Tom Kavanaugh and how he had been trained to help people and veterans overcome tremendous things in life. He strongly encouraged me to visit SSgt Kavanugh so I decided to blindly trust my brother in arms. I felt no trepidation about going to visit a stranger. My gut instinct when he mentioned Tom Kavanaugh was to book a flight and go see him as soon as possible. So the following week I jumped on a plane to go see a retired Marine named SSgt Tom Kavanaugh.

Most of you have seen the movie Star Wars so just imagine going to see Yoda and have him personally train you like Luke Skywalker. Whether I realized it or not, I was a Jedi with innate powers that I had truly never discovered. I'm going to let you in on a little secret...you have them too. You just need to find your Yoda if you haven't already. Tom is my Yoda.

You see to Marines your word is your bond and you do what you say. We do not use words like try, retreat or mission failure. Now transitioning out of the military this was a big wake up call to myself and I did get eaten by a few wolves in the process because I was about as green as you get, pretty much a sheep taking what people said at face value never questioning what was going on. This led me into some sticky financial situations I had to fight back from.

Now I gravitate to those who keep their word and look to serve others not just themselves, I call these entrepreneurs sheepdogs. Recently I was invited by a great sheepdog, John Souza, an entrepreneur who is a technology investor on a private invite only trip to fly to Cuba with over 20 entrepreneurs, all sheepdogs, that are all experts in their prospective fields. It was a surreal moment getting to bond with other entrepreneurs that were hand selected. We learned about a whole other world that seemed to be frozen in time for 50 years.

As I looked around boarding the plane to head back to the United States with this amazing group of entrepreneurs I reflected on life and how I got here. It all starts with what I say before I pray during every meal. Dear Lord allow me to be a shepherd amongst your flock and help those in need.

I've served my whole life whether it has been my family, friends, my country or the people I work with today. I only do things one way and that is all out because you practice how you play and the more you bleed in practice the less you do in war. And along the way I've had amazing coaches, mentors and teachers that continue to invest into me as I do with them. The question I would simply ask you is if you are not living the life you want and would be open to considering finding out why that is in the realms of happiness, health and wealth then what are you waiting for? Life is too short and you owe it to yourself and the ones around you that love you to step into your true genius and become someone else's hero today.

Nobody said you had to go get shot at, make game changing plays on the field or help people overcome obstacles in their own minds, you choose how to help others. That is whole beauty of being a hero. So my challenge to you is have the courage to step into your true genius where you are able to help someone else. That is truly heroism.

Why do I do what I do and get up every morning? Because I know at least 22 lives were lost the day before to veteran suicide, so that me and my children can wake up and live in a free country. Because their is a price on freedom in America everyday our military members sign a blank check and where the dollar amount goes they put in their life.

So you might be thinking right now, "what's this got to do with being a hero?" It's about the journey taken and how the twists and turns of that journey help you find your true vocation in life. I told you about my journey and how certain situations changed the trajectory of my life. I found out what I stand for and more importantly what I stand against during my journey. And in this journey I've developed a process on helping entrepreneurs overcome things around money such as money is not for me, money is bad, I'm afraid to ask for money, asking for what they feel they are worth, charging more for their services, can't get clarity on the vision of my business to name a few. I've also used this same process to work with professionals who conduct musicals on Broadway like Cats & Phantom of the Opera, professional athletes, a collegiate athlete of the year, Heisman Trophy runners, professional basketball players.

I found my true vocation is to help others truly discover their true vision in life and helping them release the invisible chains that were holding them back in their mind so they can soar to new heights like a bald eagle would well above the ground. If that makes me a hero then so it shall be it, I just consider this my calling.

I dedicate this chapter to the everyday heroes who didn't have the chance to truly say goodbye to their family and friends, may these warriors rest in peace.

SECTION 4:

SUCCESS PRINCIPLES

FIVE LESSONS

MILTON BROWN

I am sharing with you 5 lessons that I picked up from my relationship with successful people. During my life I have had many successes and many heartbreaks. I have had the opportunity to meet and build relationships with millionaires and CEOs of very successful corporations. Through these experiences I have learned valuable lessons that have helped me achieve great things. I have been able to accomplish things such as helping over 300 kids (and counting) receive free tutoring and summer camp, become Vice President of Full Charge Marketing, and discover my super power of helping others. When I look back over my life I just feel extremely blessed how far this kid from Durham, North Carolina, has come how far that I'm about to go on this journey. And I hope my life lessons from my observation and experiences of success help you in some way, shape or form.

1. They have a strong sense of SPIZZERINCTUM

I know you're probably saying "Spizzerinctum?!?! What in the world is that?" I assure you that it is a real word and no it is not a "dirty" word. This term, made famous by Ron Butler, basically means "the will to succeed." When these individuals put an idea into their head, they lock on until it comes to life. They have an unwavering resolve to push to their goal no matter how ridiculous it may seem to those who do not have their visionary eye. Once they make their decision, all or nothing with no options in between. It's amazing what happens when this unyielding decision success roots itself in someone's mind. It has literally taken the homeless to million-dollar mansions. Have you unleashed your spizzerinctum yet? Now let's look at what happens after they make their decision.

2. They take massive actions

This is where a lot of people, including myself from time to time, miss the boat. Just think about how many times you come up with a genius idea that could take your life to the next level. You become excited, because you know you have the skillset, tools, or relationships to make this work. You begin to day dream of the lifestyle changes you will be able to experience. Then you hear a ding from the microwave, grab your dinner, and your idea dies before you get to step one. You're not alone, many people find it hard to take action for multiple reasons, but mostly it's because of fear. People are so afraid to fall that they never take that first step, but not successful people. They make a plan, jump in, and figure it out along the way, and some people skip the plan stage and just jump in. How many steps have you taken on your idea? Remember, one step a day will move to closer to your goal than running away.

3. They aren't afraid of hard work.

I know you've seen the pictures of people cruising in Lamborghinis, take trips across the world, and soak up the sun on the beach on a Tuesday. You've probably heard people say man I wish I were rich so I could just goof off all day. However, people seems to miss the part where they working 100 hours a week trying to bring life in to their vision. They seem to miss the times where they live off of 3 hours of sleep, because they using the remaining 21 to create a product. They miss the sacrifices of living off of hotdogs and Raman noodles, because they want to put every available penny into their project. When it comes to observe a successful person fruits of their labor, people tend to focus solely on the fruits and completely forget about the labor.

Thomas Edison once said, "There is no substitute for hard work." Besides, searching for the easy button is just as hard as actually putting into action a proven template for success. Are you searching for an easy button?

4) They have a positive mindset.

This is a very important piece of the puzzle that I have discovered and attached onto relentless in my practice of this ideology. Have a positive mindset not only helps set into motion the "law of attraction", but it will also help you get through the darkest times on your journey towards success. I know this from experience and I treated negativity as the infectious disease it is. I remember one particular rough patch where one of my business dealings did not pan out and I was left with a negative bank account that stretched to 4 figures. However, after I had my moment of devastation I picked myself up and changed my attitude and mindset. I reminded myself that I'm in good health, I have a love family, and even though I'm in a tough spot there are still people in the world that would love to switch places with me and I should take advantage of my blessings. Long story short, I put myself back where I need to be mentally and was able to clear up that horrible situation. Having that positive mindset helped keep me going. When down it's easy to throw up your hands and give up. That's why keeping a positive attitude and mindset is important to help keep your motor running even if you're chugging through the mud. Remember, while a journey of a thousand miles may begin with the first step, you will never reach your destination if you stop moving.

5) They join masterminds.

Have you ever wondered why it seems that successful people are always able to take shortcuts? Well, here's their secret. They learn from someone that has already accomplished what they are trying to do. I'm reminded of a quote from Roy H. Williams, " A smart man makes a mistake, learns from it, and never makes that mistake again. But a wise man finds a smart man and learns from him how to avoid the mistake altogether." This is true among masterminds. I've had the opportunity to join a excellent mastermind called The Profit Coalition, and it helped me exponentially grow at an amazing rate. By joining together in a room with extremely talented and successful people with the one goal in mind to help each other succeed can take you to height you never thought possible. My life actually changed when I joined this mastermind, and through this mastermind I gained relationships that are closer than some of my family member. This mastermind is so powerful that I received my Vice President position of Full Charge Marketing by direct response to this mastermind. If you're really serious about reaching your version of success, then you should look into a mastermind that aligns itself with your same overall goal.

These five lessons may seem simple, but they pack a power so strong that they can literally change the life of whoever decides to practice them. I hope you found value from these lessons, and hope you're able to achieve the success you deserve in life. And if there is anything that I can do to help you, reach out to me and I will try my best to assist you.

DOING GOOD WHILE DOING WELL

LOU BROWN

"If it is to be - it is up to me!"

Our business inspires me!

That's a rare statement for a lot of business owners to make. But for me, it is absolutely true. I think back to when I was a kid. There are two distinct things I remember from my childhood. Money was tough, and I really had no one to fall back on.

My mom had made some bad decisions about life partners, and it ended up being just her and me against the world. Now this was back in the day when there were not a lot of government programs to help out. I'm not sure, but I don't think it would've mattered. My mother was proud, and did not really want or seek help from others.

You see, my mom was from Scotland. She came over as a war bride, and all of her family was in Scotland. We were estranged from my father, and hence, his entire family. So that just left us.

I know what it's like to have no money. I know what it's like to hide out from the rent man. My mom would say "shhh, don't say anything... I'll have the money by this weekend." She just didn't want to face anyone and have to say that.

Now I didn't know it then, but the universe was starting it's alignment with my journey in life.

I never will forget the one time we went to see some of her friends. I called them aunts and uncles, as I had none. I was about eight years old and Aunt Mabel told me a story. She said they had just bought the duplex they lived in. She told me they went to the bank, got a loan, and that the people on the other side were paying enough money in rent the cover the mortgage. What did she just say?? Even at that age I realized what she said was that they were living there for free!!

Can you imagine how that captured my imagination? Now of course, I didn't know anything about finances or money or how other people even lived. The one thing I did know was - *we* didn't have the money for rent sometimes, and *she* didn't have to pay any.

That's probably where I got the first insight that there really are parallel universes out there. Some people struggle with money and others don't. Some people put forth the effort to think and educate themselves and uncover truths that are unknown to those who do not.

Wow! So all I have to do is remember that there are people fortunate enough to apply themselves and in return, get pieces of information that allow them to break the money code.

The Money Code

The money code is quite fascinating. I am a student of it. Some people work their entire lives and end up with very little to show for it, while others seem to effortlessly move through life and always have plenty of money to spend. So, what's the difference?

I recall that my mother (God rest her soul) was one of the ones who did not take the time or gain the tools to master money -Money mastered her. I did not like the process, and saw how high interest on borrowed money could eat a fortune in a hurry.

So I watched and studied the processes involved. We visited Aunt Mabel and she told us she had bought the duplex next door and that the people on that side were paying enough in rent to cover the mortgage, with enough left over to go into their pockets. I watched their lifestyle change: a new Cadillac every other year, nice furniture, trips and cruises. And they ate out at the steakhouse almost every night!

They just kept buying real estate. One day Aunt Mabel called me and asked me to help her move. They had just bought a brand-new house. It was a two-story, all brick home, in a brand-new subdivision, on a corner lot. Far more house than she, Uncle George, and their two Chihuahuas needed.

"How did you do this, Mabel?" was my question. She said two words that changed my life: **Accumulate Property.**

Now, this parallel universe continued. When I was about 12 years old, my mother heard about a program that would allow us to buy a home. It was a modest three-bedroom home. It was very exciting and things looked positive. Then after form after form were completed and time passed, we were told that she did not qualify.

This devastated her. She didn't say much, but I could tell it really took the wind out of her sails. It was something that she wanted for me. She wanted me out of those apartments – those terrible apartments – and get me into something better, more room, a better location and in turn, a better life.

That was not to be. It affected her so badly that she never tried again.

Several years later when I was about 18 years, old Aunt Mabel said to me "hey, you need to buy a house." I said "yeah, that would be nice, Aunt Mabel, but you've bought all your property by qualifying for loans. I can't qualify my way out of a paper bag."

She laughed and said I needed to meet her friend 'Realtor Sue.' One phone call and realtor Sue was anxious to show me some property. You see, I had worked very hard during my teenage years. I had first started a paper route when I was 11 years old (actually, I was not supposed to start till 12, but I fibbed a bit.) I wanted to get ahead, and I figured this was a chance.

Every chance I got I saved up money and worked after school jobs and did other things to make things work. I knew one thing – I wanted a better life for myself and my mom.

It didn't take long until realtor Sue found a house that I liked. Turns out, I could buy this house differently than Aunt Mabel did.

Again I discovered a parallel universe: those who go to banks and qualify for loans and buy property, versus those who buy property a different way.

And the second way made all the difference.

Essentially…. it's to use the seller as the bank.

I ended up buying my first property at the age of 19, without even going to a bank or qualifying for a loan. That was a real eye-opener!

My mother became my first tenant, paying me $100 per month (along with washing some clothes and cooking some meals.) It was a good deal for me because it helped make ends meet, but it was also a good deal for her. Our rent was about $600 per month, and I told her to take $500 per month and put it towards her debt. Within a year and a half she was debt-free for the rest of her life. That was a new experience for her.

I got to see first-hand that if my mother had discovered this other universe when I was 12 years old, then I would not have spent my teenage years in an apartment.

Knowledge is power. In fact, I teach that 'Knowledge is Power *and Money*.'

As time passed, I was transferred by the company I worked for from Charlotte, North Carolina to Atlanta, Georgia. Why not? My mom was all set and the company offered to pay my closing costs if I would sell my house and buy a new one down there. So I did, and in the process I was surprised to see that in less than two years my property had gone up by 37%!

In Atlanta I again decided not to qualify for a loan, even though I could have. I told the agent to find me a house where the seller would be the bank.

Once again it happened, and to this day I have **never** qualified for a loan from a bank for a single-family or small multifamily property. There was - and is - no reason to. Why would I?

I also started to realize that if I offered my real estate the same way to the people who wanted to live there, then I could help change their lives as well. Why should they be relegated to being renters for the rest of their lives?

I could become the bank for them as the seller, and give them what I would eventually call "The Path to Home Ownership.'®

Inspiration

I started this story with "Our Business Inspires Me!" Likely now you can understand why I think so. Imagine working with a couple or a family and showing them that there is another way.

Imagine giving them a leg up in life and an opportunity that no one else has given them. Imagine working with them to help them improve their credit to the point that they can get a new loan. Or just be the bank for them and give them pride of ownership and the opportunity of possibility.

I have so many stories of people we have helped. One was a 63 years old gentleman who had never owned a home in his name in his life. He started out with our *Work for Equity Program* and did all the repairs to the home with the help of his family and friends. We credited that work towards his down payment. This allowed him the opportunity to work with a credit repair program and get his credit cleaned up so that he could get a new bank loan.

Another success story was a nurse. She loved the idea of our *Work for Equity Program* and even though she didn't have a lot of experience, she went to training sessions at the local builder supply store and learned how to do her own tile and sheet rock work. She transformed her home and made it look absolutely beautiful. We became the bank for her, and have been her bank for over five years now.

We also have a couple in the Chattanooga, Tennessee area that lived in a mobile home on her father's land for over 20 years. We had a beautiful home available on 5 acres of land, and have become the bank for these nice people for the past four years.

The stories are endless, and the challenges that human beings face are much more intense than I had to face.

People who are selling their homes are drawn to our program. They see that the home that they have enjoyed and raised their children in can be passed along through our process to a deserving family who will be raising their family there, while helping the community as well.

Whether you are a buyer, seller, lender, or real estate investor, you can likely see how it makes perfect sense to work with - and be inspired by - a Certified Affordable Housing Provider® offering the *Path To Home Ownership*® program.

Join me now and become inspired by people from throughout this country who are changing lives and making a difference in the world by 'Doing Good While Doing Well' ™.

10 PSYCHOLOGICAL TRIGGERS THAT BOOST INTERNET SALES LIKE CRAZY

NICK JAMES

A lot of marketers look at successful sales letters, and then try to mimic the words they think will boost sales. That's right, they use a swipe file. And then they wonder why their swipe-filled sales letter isn't generating many sales. Here's the thing…

If you don't understand the *psychology* of selling, then the words are going to fall flat if they're not used in the right context. If you put the components of a sales letter in the wrong order, sales will fall. If you're not pushing the right emotional sales triggers at exactly the right time, the conversion rate will be pretty abysmal.

The point is, in order to start getting more subscribers and sales, you need to understand why your prospects behave the way they do, what they're thinking, and how you can get them to act in a desired way.

That's exactly what you're about to discover within my contribution to this awesome book, as I take you by the hand and work through ten psychological sales triggers you can put to work for you starting as soon as today. You can use these triggers in your sales letters, blog posts, email marketing messages, newsletters and more. You can use them to get more subscribers, get sales, get referrals… or whatever else you need to grow your business. Sounds good, right? Let's jump in…

Sales Trigger 1: Evoke Reciprocity

Reciprocity works like this: if you give your prospects something valuable, they'll feel obligated to give you something in return. This "something" might be a referral, a sale, an email address, or something else of value to you.

The reason this works is because we tend to get psychologically uncomfortable when we feel like we owe someone something.

TIP: This doesn't work on everyone. Some people have an entitlement mentality, and you could deliver valuable stuff to their door all day long. And yet they'd have no feeling whatsoever that they owe you anything.

On the flip side, you can't be a conditional giver. In other words, you can't give with the expectation of receiving something back. So give freely and don't worry about whether others are giving you anything in return. Help your prospects, even if you aren't rewarded for it. If nothing else, this will give you a great reputation in your niche (which, in turn, will boost sales).

Let me give you a real-life example…

Let's imagine you call up a couple friends and invite them out to dinner tonight. You take them to a really nice restaurant, and everyone enjoys appetizers, a nice meal, and even dessert. When the bill comes, you snatch it off the table and insist on paying. Your friends argue a bit – after all, this was a very nice meal – but eventually they relent and then graciously thank you for the meal.

So what happens next?

If you guessed that your friends are going to take you out for dinner some night, you're absolutely right. If they didn't, they'd start to feel psychologically uneasy. Their unease would grow if you did something else nice for them in the meantime, like bought them a cup of coffee or took them out to the movies. They only way they can get rid of this psychological discomfort is by returning the favor.

Your prospects will also think the same way as your friends. If you do nice things for them, they'll feel a compulsion to return the favor.

So how can you apply this into your marketing?

The easiest way to do this is by offering a free lead magnet product, and then sending good content to your mailing list. You can also share good content on your blog and social media platforms. These simple steps will trip the reciprocity trigger.

Take note…

The key to making this work is to remind people of the trigger when you ask them for a favor.

For example: *"Since I've given you this free video, I'd like you to do a favor for me – click this link to tell your friends about the video. They're sure to love it just as much as you!"*

See how that works? You remind people what you've given them, and then you ask for what you want. It's an *"I'll scratch your back if you scratch mine"* sort of concept. And yep, it works like crazy to boost response rates. Now let's have a look at the next trigger…

Sales Trigger 2: Arouse Curiosity

Curiosity is a powerful motivator. That's because when you inject it into your content, it's like creating an itch that your readers need to scratch. And the only way they can scratch this itch is by taking some specific action *(such as joining your list or buying a product)*.

Do you ever remember the original BluBlocker sunglasses and their advertising? Marketing expert *Joseph Sugarman* eventually took over the marketing for these glasses, and they sold tens of millions of pairs. One thing Sugarman did was create curiosity in the original TV ads.

How?

By showing the reactions of real people as they looked through the sunglasses for the first time. They usually exclaimed, "Wow!" And then they'd go on to talk about how everything looked so amazing, and how they'd never worn sunglasses like this before.

Sugarman admitted that they could have slipped a BluBlocker lens over the camera lens to show the home audience what it's like to look through those sunglasses. But they didn't do it, because they wanted arouse the home audience's curiosity about what it's like to look through those glasses.

The only way to scratch that curiosity itch was to order the sunglasses by mail. It worked! The BluBlocker company sold millions of pairs of sunglasses in their first few years.

Now you too can use curiosity in your marketing. Let me give you a few examples…

Example 1: Use curiosity to ensure people keep reading.

Whether it's a blog post, email, report or even a sales letter, you can evoke curiosity in the beginning or even the middle to keep people reading until the end.

Let me give you a few specific examples:

Build anticipation in the introduction. This works really well for content such as blog posts, newsletter articles and reports. Simply tell people what they're going to learn in the report or article, and arouse curiosity in the process.

For example: You'll find out what exercise the world's most elite militaries have used for 500 years to train their best soldiers!

Tell a story, but don't quite finish it. This arouses emotion, which is a good thing. But if you don't finish the story right away, it also arouses curiosity.

For example: So you're probably wondering if Jane met her goal and lost 50 pounds. You know what? I think the results are really going to surprise you. I'll tell you all about them in just a few minutes. But first, let me share with you the #1 mistake dieters make that stalls your progress…

Whet their appetite for what's coming. You can do this anywhere in a sales letter, article or report.

For example: Jane got amazing fat-loss results using the same secret your favorite Hollywood celebrities use when they need to shed the fat fast. You'll discover this secret in just a moment. But first…

Example 2: Make people curious about a product.

Let's say you're selling a book about how to get traffic. You might arouse curiosity by saying something like this:

You'll discover the closely guarded traffic source that's never been revealed before – just wait till you see how much traffic it brings!

You can bet anyone who is interested in getting more traffic will be a bit curious about this little-known traffic source.

Here's another example that would make a great benefit statement in a bulleted list:

You'll find out which common herb reduces fine lines and wrinkles – you may already have it in your cupboard! *(See page 15 to find out what it is.)*

So you can see how this all works. Make people curious, and you'll keep them hooked on your content, joining your list and buying your product just to satisfy their curiosity. Now the next powerful sales trigger…

Sales Trigger 3: Be Specific

People are always a little skeptical whenever they're reading bold claims in ads or other content. However, there are ways to reduce their skepticism and make them more likely to believe what you're telling them. One of these ways is by being specific about your claims.

The best way to explain this is with an example. Take a look at these two statements:

Statement 1: You'll find out how Jorge made $5000 last month with Facebook ads, and how you can too!

Statement 2: You'll find out how Jorge made $5223 last month with Facebook ads, and how you can too!

Those statements are exactly the same, except for the dollar amount. The first one is an even $5000, whereas the second statement is very specific.

Guess which statement is more compelling?

If you guessed Statement 2, you're right. That's because it's highly unbelievable that someone made exactly $5000 last month. It's far more believable that they made $5223. Because the claim is specific, it seems more believable.

This doesn't just work for dollar amounts – it works for most anything where you can be specific about a number. This includes:

Length of time. For example, "31 days" is more specific than "one month."

Weight. "Jack lost 63.5 pounds" is more specific and believable than "Jack lost 60 pounds."

Other dimensions such as length and width. "The plants grew 13 inches tall" is more specific and believable than saying they "grew about a foot."

Number. For example, "15,955 subscribers" is more specific and believable than "about 16,000 subscribers."

So you get the point. Whenever you can be specific about a number or any other detail, do so because people are more likely to believe specific claims. Now the next trigger…

Sales Trigger 4: Handle Objections

If you're selling something, then your prospects are already figuring out reasons why they shouldn't buy it. These are called objections.

Common objections include the following…

The price is too high. Here the person may be able to afford the product or service, but he still thinks the price is high compared to the value you've demonstrated.

You can fix this by demonstrating more value *(sharing benefits)* and clearly stating your USP *(unique selling position)*. You can also specifically give people a reason why the price is so high.

For example:

The price for this inner circle membership is higher than what you've seen elsewhere, because we only want serious business owners in this elite group.

TIP: Want to see how to justify high prices? Then start reading ads for luxury goods and services, such as Rolex, Mercedes, Bentley, Armani and similar goods. In most cases, you'll see the price justification is based around their branding and USP.

The price is too low. Low prices are sometimes equated with the product or service being "cheap" or "junk," so this objection makes people wonder why you'd price the item so low. That's why you need to justify low prices, too.

For example:

I know what you're thinking – this price is crazy low! You might even be thinking something is missing from this package.

Nope, you get the FULL course for a fraction of the price.

Why?

It's because I want to make this course affordable to everyone. It's not fair if only rich people can afford this course. So for a limited time you can get this course for a song – but hurry before this special offer ends!

I can't afford it. This objection isn't that the price is too high, but rather that the prospect is thinking he shouldn't spend his money on that particular item right now. Sometimes that may be true. Sometimes that's just an objection you need to handle because it's nothing more than an excuse.

The solution? Justify the price. A good way to do this is to compare it to other activities or products, which show why your product is a good value.

For example:

If you hired a ghostwriter to create this report, you'd pay at least $750 for it. But if you're one of the first 100 people to act now and get a PLR license, you get full rights to this report for $50. You can't afford to pass up this steal of a deal!

Another example is to point out how the item is comparable to some small thing the person regularly purchases.

For example:

You get this complete report for the price of a small pizza. You won't find a better way to invest $9, so click the order button below now.

I'm not sure if it will work for me. For this objection you simply offer a guarantee (AKA risk reversal).

For example:

I'm so confident you'll love this product that I'm willing to back this offer with an iron-clad 100% money back guarantee. If you're unsatisfied for any reason whatsoever, simply email me and I'll promptly issue a full refund... no questions asked.

So you can see how this works. Be sure to handle those common objections you just learned about. However, you need to take it a step further: you'll need to examine your specific product and figure out what people might object to so you can handle those objections as well. Next trigger...

Sales Trigger 5: Build Credibility

Whenever your prospects are reading your sales letter or other content, they've got their defense shields up. They're skeptical. And one of the thoughts that will be floating through their head is this: "Why should I listen to this person?"

You need to give your prospects a good reason. In other words, you need to build your credibility.

Let me give you some examples of credibility-building statements:

Why should you listen to me? Simple: because last year my business generated $1,117,922. I know how marketing works, and now I want to share my secrets with you.

I lost 50 pounds using this diet plan, and I've kept it off for three years. I've helped 388 other people just like you lose at least 50 pounds too. This plan worked for me, it works for others, and it will work for you too.

My books have soared to the top of the USA Today Bestseller's lists three times in the past 18 months – so you know this novel-writing course is the real deal.

I've spent ten years honing my copywriting skills. My sales letters have pulled in $10 million worth of frontend sales and created countless backend opportunities. Now you too can put my experience and skills to work for you.

Dr. Simon has spent the last two decades learning everything there is to know about the human metabolism. You won't find a better-researched book or a medical doctor with more experience in this field.

So the bottom line here is to give your readers a reason to listen to you. Do you have experience? Credentials? A degree? Specific results in the field? Awards?

Whatever it is, build your credibility by sharing it with your readers.

Next up...

Sales Trigger 6: Use Social Proof

Here's something to understand about your prospects...

They're unsure of themselves. They're not sure what to do. They prefer to see what others are doing, and then follow along.

That's right, people tend to be a little conformists.

I'm not making this up. Scientists have proven that people like to conform with others.

For example, let me ask you which line is longer:

Line A: ---------------

Line B: --------------------------

There's no question, right? Obviously Line B is longer. You can show these lines to anyone with normal vision, and they'll all tell you that Line B is longer.

So let's imagine you have a guy named Joe who's judging line length. There are three other people in the room who are also judging line length, and all three of them say that "Line A" is longer. These three people are shills – they work for the researcher. After Joe hears all these other people say Line A is longer, he now has to give his answer.

Guess what? Joe is more likely to say "Line A" is longer, even though you can see it in his face that he knows that's not true. He is simply conforming with the group because it makes him feel more psychologically comfortable to go along with what everyone else is doing and saying. *(Hint: This is why "peer pressure" makes such a big impact on people.)*

You can use this tendency to conform in your sales process. All you have to do is show your prospects that everyone else is buying your product, joining your mailing list, or "liking" your social media posts. This is called social proof.

Let me give you specific examples:

Testimonials. Your prospects don't always believe you (they figure you're biased), which is why testimonials work so well to boost sales. What's more, testimonials help trip that conformity factor as well, which also pushes people towards the conformity button.

Tickers. This is where you show people buying a product or joining your site in a live ticker. Of course you can't share specifics, but you might have something such as "John from London just joined... Suzy from California just joined..." If you have a lot of sales, subscribers or registrations coming in each day, it's a powerful way to use social proof to further boost your conversion rate.

Numbers. Think of how McDonald's Restaurant signs used to say things such as, "Over one billion hamburgers served." That's social proof using numbers.

Social media has social proof built right in. For example, anyone visiting your Facebook Page can see how many fans you have, and how many people like, share or comment on your posts.

You can share other numbers as well, such as how many customers you have, how many subscribers, etc. E.G., "3287 satisfied customers can't be wrong, so order now!"

So here's the bottom line: show your prospects and visitors that OTHER people are buying your products, subscribing to your newsletter, following you on social media, and other activities. This social proof will get even more people doing the same thing. Next up...

Sales Trigger 7: Invoke Fear

Fear is an incredibly powerful motivator. You'll see everyone from marketers to politicians to bosses to parents using fear to get people to take some specific action. They do it because it works.

Now, I'm not saying you have to act like *Freddy Krueger* from the horror movies and scare the heck out of your prospects. Not at all. Instead, all you have to do is lightly touch the fear trigger to make a big impact.

Here's how to do it...

Create a Fear of Missing Out

This phrase *(fear of missing out)* has become so popular recently that it has its own acronym: FOMO. Typically this applies to people who can't stop looking at their smartphones, because they have a fear of missing out on some Facebook post, pop culture trend, or even an invitation to go out.

You can take this natural fear and funnel it into your sales system by creating an offer that's somehow limited. For example:

Limit the offer to a set number of people. For example, perhaps you set up a membership site with a strict membership limit of just 250 people. Or you can offer a bonus or discount to the next 100 people who order now.

Offer a discount or bonus for a limited amount of time. For example, you can offer a 50% discount that ends in 72 hours.

As you can see, there are a lot of different ways to create scarcity, boost urgency and in general create a sense of fear. These include:

- Coupons.
- Discount sales.
- Flash sales.
- Dime sales *(the price goes up every day or after every purchase)*.
- Early bird offers.
- Introductory special rates.
- Holiday sales.
- Grand opening sales.

I could go on with this list. In all cases, the offer is somehow limited. This creates a fear of missing out on a great deal, which in turn boosts your conversion rate.

Here's the second way to create fear...

Remind People of Their Fears

One of the best examples of this comes from the marketing you see from insurance companies. Basically, they get prospects to imagine what it would be like if they lost everything in a fire... and they didn't have insurance.

You don't need to sell insurance to remind people of their fears. No matter what you're selling, you can remind people of what might happen if they don't order now. For example:

If you choose to do nothing and leave this sales page, you won't lose the weight. The ridicule will continue. People will give you disapproving looks when you're out on the street. You'll hate what you see when you look in the mirror.

This problem is not going to get better if you ignore it. Those few fleas you see on your dog now will multiply. Soon your entire house will be infested. Fleas will infiltrate the carpet, the furniture and even your bed.

You see how this works? Create a scarce offer or remind people of their fears, and you'll see a boost to your conversion rate. Now the next conversion-boosting triggers…

Sales Trigger 8: Radiate Authority

You've probably heard of the old Stanley Milgram psychology studies, where average people were told by an authority figure – which was a researcher in a white coat -- to deliver electric shocks to someone else whom they couldn't see.

Of course there weren't real shocks being delivered, but the subjects of this experiment didn't know that. They were told the shocks were real, and they could even hear someone screaming and pleading in the next room over not to shock them. Yet these research subjects kept delivering shocks… all because an authority figure told them to do so.

I'm not suggesting you run around trying to get people to deliver electric shocks to others. Rather, you can use any authority you might possess to help build your credibility, get people to listen to you, and get people to do what you want.

Here's how…

State Your Credentials

If you have some position of authority in your niche, then be sure others know about your credentials. This might be a degree or career path, such as doctor, lawyer or law enforcement. If you have a photo to back this up – such as you in judge's robes or a uniform – include this with your content.

Borrow Other People's Authority

If you don't have a position of authority, you can still use authority to your advantage by borrowing other people's position of authority. How? By doing joint ventures or even just getting testimonials from authority figures.

For example, maybe you have a diet guide. You can have medical doctors and nutritionists review it and offer their testimonials.

TIP: This is like the advertisements where they state something like, "four out of five dentists agree." That's using borrowed authority to boost sales.

Radiate Authority

You don't have to have any specific credentials in order to position yourself as an authority in your niche. If you're an expert, then act like one. Be a strong leader. For example:

Speak (write) with confidence. The more confident you sound in your articles, sales letters, blog posts and other content, the more likely it is people will follow you without question.

Position yourself as an authority. Basically, this means blanketing your niche with content. Write guest blog posts. Write and publish a book. Give talks. The more people see your excellent content, the more they'll associate you with an authority in a niche.

So the bottom line is so establish yourself as an authority, show your credentials when applicable, and borrow other people's authority when possible. Together, these tactics will boost your conversion rate. Next up…

Sales Trigger 9: Be Honest

I know it seems like common sense that you should be honest. But the truth is, a lot of people seem to think that marketers and sales people aren't honest. Just ask anyone what their impressions are of used-car dealers. That's an entire profession where everyone tends to be lumped into the "dishonest" pile. Those writing ads of any kind aren't far behind.

Of course sales people don't help their own image. While the vast majority don't tell outright lies, many of them skirt around the truth with "errors of omission." In other words, these marketers and sales people don't let prospects know what's wrong with the product.

Now here's a trick to really boost your conversion rate: be honest with your prospects, tell them all about the flaws, and then turn these perceived flaws into assets.

Just the fact that you're being honest about a product or service is going to make people trust you more, which in turn boosts sales.

However, the other part of this is that you're handing an objection by turning a perceived flaw into an asset. As you learned earlier in this report, handing objections is another good way to boost your conversion rate.

Let me give you a real life example of turning a liability or flaw into an asset.

Listerine is a mouthwash that's known for having a strong taste. Scope *(a mouthwash competitor)* directly attacked Listerine by saying that using Scope produces fresh breath without "medicine mouth."

So now Listerine is having a perception problem in that prospects think their product is going to taste yucky, like medicine. Listerine responds with ads that say this: "Listerine: You can handle it. Germs can't."

Boom! Listerine is basically saying in these ads that the strong taste is what kills the germs. And by inference, they're saying that any mouthwash that doesn't have a strong taste probably isn't killing germs.

See how that works? Listerine didn't hide the fact that they have a strong-tasting mouthwash. Instead, they turned that perceived weakness into a strength of the product by suggesting their product tastes strong because it kills germs.

Now you can boost your conversion rates and sales using this same strategy. Simply be honest no matter what you're selling *(your product or an affiliate product)*, and turn perceived flaws into assets whenever possible.

For example, maybe you're selling an eBook that seems a bit thin compared to other ebooks on the topic. Some people might feel like they're not getting their money's worth if the book is too short. You can turn this perceived flaw into an asset by saying this book is for busy people – there's no fluff, no filler, just meat.

So go ahead and think about what's wrong with your products and the affiliate products you're selling. Don't hide these flaws in your sales copy and product reviews. Instead, put 'em front and center, and turn the perceived flaws into strengths. Next up…

Sales Trigger 10: Evoke Consistency

People don't want to view themselves as wishy-washy flip-floppers who change their mind whenever the wind blows. People like to view themselves as consistent and committed. You can use this psychological fact to boost your sales.

How? By using the *foot in the door* technique.

It works like this…

You get your "foot in the door" by getting your prospect to perform some small action or do you some small favor. Then later you ask them for a bigger favor. Since they want to appear consistent, they're likely to do your bigger favor.

Researchers have examined this psychological trigger, and they've found it truly works. Researchers started by asking people in a neighborhood to put a big, ugly sign in their front yard. Naturally, the vast majority of people said no.

Then these researchers did a test with another group of folks. They asked this second group to put a small placard in their window that promoted picking up trash or some other neutral activity. Many people said yes, because it was an easy way to support beautifying the neighborhood.

A couple weeks later, researchers returned to those who displayed the placard and asked if they'd also display a yard sign. You got it – that yard sign was the big, ugly one. And you know what? A whole bunch of these people said yes because they wanted to remain consistent.

So here's the point: if you ask for a big favor right away, people will outright say no. But ask them for a small, easy favor first to get your foot in the door, and these folks are more likely to say yes when you ask for a bigger favor later.

For example:

Ask people to join your mailing list first *(easy favor),* and then later ask them to buy your entry-level product.

Ask people to buy your entry-level product, then ask them to buy your home study course.

Offer an upsell to those who're in the process of buying your course.

Ask people who've "liked" your social media content to share it with their friends.

Propose a small, easy joint venture with a partner first, and then later propose a bigger joint venture project.

Ask your prospects to enter your free contest, and then later ask them to register for a webinar.

You get the idea. Get your foot in the door with small requests and see if you too don't get a bigger response rate when you make larger requests.

Now let's wrap things up…

Conclusion

What you've learned in this section of the book is like pulling back the curtain to see how the world's best sales people, internet marketers and politicians seem to almost magically lead people to do what they want. And now you too can boost your sales and response rates by employing the following ten psychological sales triggers:

1. Reciprocity
2. Curiosity
3. Specificity
4. Objection-Handling
5. Credibility
6. Conformity
7. Fear
8. Authority
9. Honesty
10. Consistency

Now the key here is not to cherry pick through these methods and merely use a few of them. Instead, put as many of these methods to work for you every time you write a sales letter, publish a newsletter, post something on your blog, or write any other type of persuasive content.

These are extremely powerful triggers that researchers have proved time and again work like crazy to boost your response rates. But don't take my word for it – try them for yourself to see what kind of results you'll get. I think you'll be amazed!

TWELVE STEPS TO SUCCESS
WITH A SUBSCRIPTION WEB SITE

TOM CONE

Use this checklist to see if your subscription web site idea has what it takes to be a success.

1. The site must offer a unique 'experience' and information unavailable anywhere else on the net. This usually means original material written from a unique perspective. If there have other sites that offer free material recently written by this same author, it can dilute the value of the subscription site.

The winning concept is "if the visitor to your site wants to read this material, then the only way to do so is to become a subscriber to your site." If potential subscribers believe the same material is available free elsewhere, they will not join.

2. The site must target a very narrow niche market with very specific information on a tightly focused subject. It is far better to have a topic that hits the 'hot button' of just 5000 people who are intensively interested, even emotionally involved, with your topic, that it is to have a topic that 'everyone is interested in', but no one is emotionally involved with. Keep in mind that most people make buying decisions based on emotion, not logic. Make sure your subscription web site topic has a strong emotionally (as well as logical) appeal to potential subscribers.

3. The site must offer a sense of community. Potential subscribers should be made aware that there is a strong community of people who come together at this one site to share information, thoughts and opinions on this one topic which they are emotionally involved with. They need to know that when they become members of this community, they will be able to network with others in this community (through a discussion group).

4. The site must offer a sense of exclusivity. Potential subscribers should feel that by joining the site they will be joining an exclusive club (similar to a gated community), where only those inside the gates get to share the benefits of the gated community. Knowing that joining the site adds them to an 'exclusive club' with benefits not available to the masses, adds to the perceived value and appeal of the site.

5. The site must have a 'group leader'. The site needs a 'captain of the ship' who pulls the community together, keeps it focused on the subject matter, and provides a continual supply of updated information that keeps subscribers coming back.

6. The site must have a 'compelling reason to join' - Even if you have all the above going for you, unless your site gives a potential visitor a 'compelling reason to join', they probably won't join. They'll just file the site as 'interesting', and then go on their way. Ideally you want your visitor to say, "This is exactly what I have been looking for!

I want to join immediately!" If you can create that kind of feeling in your targeted market, you will do well.

7. The site must follow a viable business model - If your business model requires 5000 paying members in order to break even, you are probably doomed to failure before you start. But if you have low overhead, and need only a small number of members to be profitable you have a much better chance of success.

8. The look of the site must be immediately appealing to your visitors Too many sites are confusing, have no overall theme, are difficult to navigate, and scream 'amateur'. When visitors reach your site, they should immediately feel comfortable with what they see. Anything else gives them a reason to head for the exits.

9. Every element on the site should give visitors a subconscious reason to join the site. Fine tune the site so that every element (especially on the front pages) gives the visitor another reason to join.

Do this by having departments and article headlines that include intriguing hot button' headlines. Have interesting content teaser copy that just begs to be clicked. When departments or articles are clicked, the visitor already has a reason to join - to see the content they clicked. That's when to display the 'join us' page.

If the visitor has come to your site, it is usually because they are looking for the information you offer. Make sure your main page gives them a good impression of what is within your site. Avoid the hard sell - let your content do the work for you.

10. The site must be easy for you to build and maintain. If done by manual coding, maintaining a content rich subscription web site can be very time consuming. Add in time required to review and process all the elements of the subscription side, and the time requirements could easily exceed your resources. You can eliminate this problem by using an fully automatic content management and subscription web site publishing tool.

11. The site must have password sharing blocking - If a member posts their user name and password on a discussion board or news group, you could have thousands of unauthorized visitors a day using that password to get into your site. To prevent this, you must have an automated procedure to detect and immediately disable member accounts that are being used inappropriately. Ideally, your subscription web site management and publishing tool will do this for you.

12. The site must have readily available reporting tools - Knowing what is going on within your subscription web site is the quickest way to find and resolve problems, and provide better content to current and potential subscribers. Reports should show you where your visitors are coming from, what they are looking for, what they search for, and in general, what is going on at any moment, as well as history and developing trends at your site. And of course, you should be able to view all income transactions and all site activity records quickly.

If you get the above twelve items on the above checklist right, you will greatly increase your chances of success with your own 'Membership' web site.

But if you get just one of them wrong, you can expect problems, some quite severe.

BECOMING A MARKETING HERO ON MOBILE!

TONY MC CARTHY

In over three decades in marketing, I have seen the advent of the fax machine, the Computer, the laptop, the internet, however never before have I seen such an abundance of opportunity as in marketing on mobile devices.

I started my marketing journey at the age of 17 when I was given a tile brochure, by my father and was told "Go Sell These!" Yes. I am one of the old guard who believe that good marketing, leads to good sales and great marketing leads to greater sales. However I digress, my marketing journey has gone for brick and mortar stores, from B to B, B to C and back again. My single largest sale was for $6.5 million Dollars and never have I been so excited at the possibility of mobile.

A number of years back, I feel in love with Internet marketing, being able to market to anyone who is connected by a computer really excited me. Then a event happened which would change my marketing direction forever. A friend of mine (Matt Bacak) and I were hanging in my house with my family and his, he had come over to kiss the Blarney stone. After we had eaten we started talking about making a mobile app, a game actually. It was about a leprechaun, who gets kicked in the butt and gives out to you. Oh yeah and shoots rainbows out his butt as well. Well we made the app, it was Called Leapin' Leprechaun and went to 38 in the iTunes store in the USA. I was hooked on mobile.

Matt returned to his online marketing world. I made numerous apps and then my marketing brain kicked in. To look for opportunities within the market, where are the sweet spots. First let's look at the impact of the smartphone.

In the history of mankind there never has been a piece of technology that has become so personal to people than the mobile device. You sleep with it, wake with it, and will never leave home without it. Ask yourself this, would you loan you mobile to anyone for 24 hours? Or would you feel someway naked without it. Actually we are more likely to leave home without our wallets now than our mobile phone. Now the smart device is an appendage to the human form. So how do you become a marketing hero?

First we must understand the sociology impact of the smart device that is the smart phone has become 'mine'. It's my phone! It has bridged the divide been personal item and technology in a way that no one could have foreseen. It is now a phone, a computer and a way to communicate in numerous different ways. The important part of this, is its how I want, when I want, and the way that I want. For marketers and brand manager this is where the opportunity and challenges are!

Before we delve into that opportunities and challenges and how you can be a superhero on mobile, we need a quick look at how the mobile eco system is dived. We all know apps are the way we engage on mobile and app mentality has been clearly defined, that is, an app must have one core function and no more. Look at industry giants like Facebook, they separated their chat app from their newsfeed app, google separated email from calendar from YouTube etc. App mentality means is fast simple and single focused.

The challenge for us marketers and brand managers is how we engage with the market in such a fragmented eco system. We know that people still ask "Dr. Google" as in search, the same way as on a desktop, however they are engaging with social media much more frequently. In a recent survey people admitted that while out in a restaurant they will use the restroom more frequently, in order to check their social media accounts.

So how do you become a SUPERHERO at mobile marketing? Here are some top tips to do that…

> You need to communicate with the market via multiple touch points, that is in simple terms, in the way they want to talk, either email, Facebook, snapchat etc. etc. Or using multiple strands at one time. This means you need to get the user to willing give you their ids on multiple different accounts, not just email, Facebook, twitter etc.

> The experience must be the same across platform. Not just mobile enable web sites, but responsive. So that the experience is the same, no matter what device the user engages with you on.

> Don't ask them to Type. Make all logins social responsive.

> Don't, ask them to download any pdfs or files. Phones have small memory, I will not give up space.

Top TIP: Mobile marketing is a tool in the marketing war chest, you cannot market on any one single device, channel or social medium anymore.

They are many more tips and updates you can find at **htpp://anthonymccarthy.com**, however for now let's go on a journey that I discovered by accident. While doing a mobile based project for Logitech to increase their brand awareness, I came across a very large unfair advantage for building a list. You see, most people cannot build a list from mobile: Fact, however I discovered a system that not only allows you to build a list, but will grow your social media. The amazing part of this system is that the market actually brings in more people to your list and grow your social media for you.

Why a list, well that's the internet marketing secret, ever marketer/company/brand that are crushing it have a list, from Netflix to all the guys in this book. Any email subscriber is worth anything from 0.50 per month to $75 dollars depending on your business or market niche.

Now in today's marketing world you need to communicate with people on the platform they want to talk to you on, that's a fact. However email is still one of the most effective way to communicate, you need also to communicate with your market on multiple channels. Sounds like a lot of work right! Well the good news is not anymore.

With the buildmylistnow.net program that I have developed with my partner Nick James (internet Marketer of The year!) you can have all the channels covered by your market, that's right, the market will talk about YOU!. You can also have a huge email list, to email your market and tell them about your products, other people's products.

Our BuildMyListNow.net list-building program is getting rave reviews from seasoned Internet Marketers as well as from college students, stay-at-home moms and retired grandparents. In the BuildMyListNow.net system he outlines a step-by-step plan that is simple to follow, yet incredibly powerful when it comes to generating new leads for any business.

IN THE STACKS

SHERMAN RAGLAND

It was Christmas 1997, and my fledgling consulting, investment banking business, whatever you want to put on it, had just got started. I just closed the biggest deal ever for one of my clients. They had actually made a $100 million off of what I'd done for them. They sent me a really nice package, and in that package was a beautiful note telling them how much they appreciated me and how much I'd done for them, and also enclosed was a fruitcake. $100 million, fruitcake. I got mad, not at them. I was mad at me, because here I had worked for IBM and worked for Xerox and worked for the biggest developer in Washington DC and basically had spent all this time making other people very, very wealthy, and I promised myself when I opened that business I was going to be in it for me. I was going to do things for me, and here I was slipping back into these same old habits I was doing as an employee, and truthfully I felt like a fraud.

I wasn't an entrepreneur. I was just trading hours for dollars. The thing I have to share with you, which is why it felt so bad for me, is because just 14 years earlier, I was the kid on campus that everybody hated. I had three jobs. I worked really, really, really hard, really hard, because I came up from a deficit. I'd actually start off as a music major and switched to business and worked really, really hard. People say, "Hey Sherman, let's go to this party. Let's go to that party," I'm like, "No. I got to go to work. I got to study. Got to work, study, go to work."

The reward for working really, really hard was that when I graduated, I actually had a fellowship to the business school of my choice. I picked Wharton, so don't you all be hating on me. I picked Wharton, and there I was literally the very first day of class, the very first week of class, and I get this knock on the door. I said, "Hey, the door's open. Come on in." It was my brand new friend Terrance.

Terrance and I had met in student orientation and we instantly bonded. I mean, he was literally like my long-lost twin brother. In almost every respect, we were very, very similar. He had just graduated. I had just graduated. We were very, very similar except in one regard. My family had struggled with money issues for generations. I'm the grandson of a West Virginia coal miner who picked up when my dad was 8 years old and said to my dad and to my aunt and to my grandmother, "I'm leaving."

My dad was first generation to go to college, so we struggled with money issues because we didn't know anything about money. Terrance on the other hand, by almost every single measure, his family was rich. In fact, his father was a very well-known ophthalmologist up in the New Jersey area. He had a couple of optometry stores, and he had vested very, very well. In fact, I found out much later Terrance's family actually owned a 10 bedroom mansion that had formerly belonged to the Colgate family, the Colgate-Palmolive family in this gated community.

Terrance comes knocking on my door. He comes into my room, and he says, "Hey.

What are you doing?" I said, "I'm studying, getting ready to think. Go get something to eat." "Get something to eat! Come on. Let's go to the library." I'm like, "Go to the library? Why do I want to do that?" He says, "I want to go to the stacks." "Go to the stacks. What's that?" He said, "Just come with me."

He hauled me over to the library, and there for the first time in my life, I went inside this library that was really all about business. It was quite literally the cathedral of capitalism. Amen. There was books literally from the floor to the ceiling all about business and how to make business decisions, how to grow a business, and books and magazines and papers.

Terrance and I rolled up our sleeves and quite literally for 2 years, we did research looking to answer one question. How do you make it in America? How do you create wealth in America, not just for yourselves, but literally for your children's children? On that day that I was so ticked off, I knew I had betrayed what I had learned and what was ultimately to become my ministry, sharing what I learned in the Wharton Business School that has traditionally been locked out to many people who look like me, locked out to people who just, you know, they're also grandsons and granddaughters of coal miners.

What we learned during that 2 years ... Terrance ultimately went on and became the dean of a very famous business school, but what we learned was really 4 things, real quick. Number 1, all wealth in America is created 1 way, a great idea implemented well. Number 2, you need a business vehicle to implement that idea. Number 3, you need mentors and masterminds to help you grow your business. Number 4, you need real estate. You need real estate, because all of us are going to wake up one day and say, "You know what? As much as we've loved this, I don't want to do this anymore." The only way you're going to be able to walk away from that business for most of us, and still maintain your lifestyle, is to have a passive income stream, and yes, there really is some magic in real estate.

I could go on and on and on, but I don't have time to do that, so what I'd love to do is just give you a copy of my book. It's called, "Wealth we can!" You can get it at wealthwecan.org.

[From a speech given to the Entrepreneurs' Student's Club at the Harvard Business Club.]

USING OUR GREATEST WEAKNESS AS AN ONLINE STRENGTH

Alex Arnold.

Understanding modern behavior is the reason that all marketing companies make millions – they research people's greatest fears, wants, desires and motivations and based on that, they develop a product (whether useful or not) and sell it to us knowing that we will be compelled to get it.

On that note, all human beings have a weakness that is constantly played on, not all of them will admit it but unfortunately according to science – it's inherent. If over time, you have learned to not care about this particular weakness or have overcame it – just know this – the millions of others that haven't will be your client base.

Besides, it is not a weakness if used properly. Ethically. Smart people know that weaknesses can become strengths.

So what is this little catch in human behavior that affects most of us?

Here's a clue dating back to ancient Greece. In Greek mythology, there was a God, one you will have heard of – his name was **Narcissus**.

He was a hunter from <u>Thespiae</u> in Boeotia who was known for his physical beauty and the son of the river god <u>Cephissus</u>. He was a very proud creature who rejected most of those who loved him.

Nemesis noticed this behavior and thought it rather mean and so devised a plan. He attracted Narcissus to a nearby pool, where Narcissus saw his own reflection in the water for the first time and fell in love with it, not realizing it was simply an image.

Unable to leave the beauty of his reflection, Narcissus lost his will to live. He became addicted to his own image. He stared at his reflection until the day that he died. Narcissus, as you know, is the origin of the term *narcissism*, a fixation with oneself and one's physical appearance. I'm sure we know a few people just like him.

However, here's the truth – we *all* have a fixation with our image. With the dawn of the recent 'selfie' craze, you cannot fault the logic. Everyone likes to see themselves experiencing something good or looking their best. Not just our faces and our bodies which we constantly try to improve, but also with how people see us, how we see ourselves and how eager we are to show off the things that we have and do. This is our weakness. Self-love is wonderful don't get me wrong but pre-occupation with our own image when used incorrectly or obsessively leads us to buy things we don't want to impress people we don't like, with money we don't have. It's a dangerous path. But it can be used to our advantage, especially in business. And very especially online.

Here are a few secrets to selling more products and getting more awareness just by using this knowledge:

- **Be socially present**. People like to compare – they want to know if you are doing better, what you are doing and mostly if you can help them be a better 'image' version of themselves with your services. So *be* there. Ensure that you are advertising on all of the channels available including Facebook and most of all Instagram. Not many Internet Marketers are Instagramming. They think 'it's just a bunch of pictures'. But pictures can paint a thousand words and are often more effective than a long spiel. Instagram is bigger than you think and is a very simple marketing strategy. If used in the right way, you can let the pictures you post reflect the image that you want to project in conjunction with whatever you are selling and you don't even have to do much writing apart from a few good hashtags and a link to your products.

• **Sell discreetly.** Be careful that you do not *openly* sell on these channels – people hate that. You must come across like a decent, normal person with an ongoing life and an objective other than making money. Use your self-love to get out there and show yourself off as a personal person. This is why Instagram works wonders. Say for example you are selling a business opportunity for people to make more money. Instead of stating a big long list of reasons as to why they should invest in you – show them pictures. Show yourself with lots of free time on a beach, get a high quality camera and be interesting with your images. If people want that life– they can click the link. It's subtle and it's clever because no one wants to be less or to feel left out. Plus it plays on the need for them to upgrade their image, to be more pro-active and your pictures are evidence that it is achievable. They want to be there, they want to take those pictures and you might be the vehicle to get them there. No massive video scripts needed here. Of course, if talking is what you are good at, play to your strengths. Use YouTube, use your website and just be yourself, not a sales person.

• **Understand human behavior.** Now that you know people want to constantly upgrade themselves and improve their image – give them what they want. Invest in products that create that feel-better feeling. This is your avenue to plenty of clients. Give constant reinforcement that what you have is what they want. They know it – so it's time for you to know it.

Remember, we all have a little Narcissus in us and we don't need a pool to get people to look at themselves and decide that they can use us to improve their experience. If you don't sell it, someone else will.

SECTION 5:

INSPIRATION & MOTIVATION

ALL ABOUT CHOICES

HELGA ZELINSKI

Every day, every minute we make choices. Choices about immediate actions, planning the next step or the future. These choices can have far reaching effects and can be responsible to change the rest of your life and that of future generations.

We make decisions and choices in split seconds to keep us safe and secure. Choices to react to our surroundings and to others in what we consider an appropriate manner. Some of the everyday simple choices include what food to eat, what clothes to wear and our overall image we present to the rest of the world.

When faced with simple options, and one being advantages over the other, the choices are clear and immediate and are just part of every day's routine. We are usually satisfied with the outcome and move on to the next issue.

Practice, experience and gut feelings can help with everyday decisions but what about the more difficult choices such as choosing a partner for life, planning to have children, which car to buy, where to live, investing in real estate or other commodities and to evaluate job opportunities.

Making good choices can be complicated. Some tasks can be solved intellectually others may be solved by going with your gut feeling. The decision-making process on a day to day, minute to minute basis can be very simple or become more difficult as the issues become more complicated.

With more choices, it becomes harder to decide since the consequences are more severe and may have far reaching implications. The more important decisions often allow us to work through the details and we can evaluate the pros and cons and the consequences our choices may present.

Many people procrastinate or make no decision at all, leaving it up to chance and if the outcome is unsatisfactory they blame it on everything else except their own inability to make decisions. Hoping for the best is not a good option and luck should only play a small part in the outcome. A decision well thought out and executed is giving you confidence and satisfaction.

So- why are we not able to create the perfect life if we make perfect choices? Why do bad things happen to good people?

Many people have questioned their faith when it came to understanding why bad things, such as sickness, disasters or misfortunes happen to good people. Why are children, which are the most vulnerable and innocent beings, born with challenges and struggles to survive?

We see good people suffering from the most serious diseases such as cancer, being taken advantage of by charlatans and criminals and are presented with major challenges throughout their lives.

Do we get what we deserve, does honesty and a desire to do the right thing have a place in this society? Does hard work and dedication lead to rewards and job promotions? Do values and integrity still matter?

Sadly, this is not always the case. To receive rewards for their honest efforts is dependent on many factors. Even making the right choices for their own well-being, your families and communities is not a guarantee to success and prosperity.

The big picture here is that we are part of a family, a community, a country and humanity in general. Our circle of influence extends to and has the most impact on the individuals closest to you and in turn their decisions and choices are most critical to your own day to day life.

Some of the most important choices are the partner you choose to spend your life with and raise a family together. The type of work or profession you choose which will have an impact on your lifestyle income and overall satisfaction level and should be tailored to your preferences to fill a position in the arena of health, business or a more free-spirited environment

On a larger scale, we are part of political movements by casting our votes for candidates of potential leaders and the future of legislative changes and their impact on society.

Choosing a leader is one of the most important decisions we can make. This leader should be representing our interests for security, moral standards, fair taxation, positioning on international levels and to provide a prosperous economy.

At the same time, we are influenced by the actions of others and areas we cannot control, such as climate change, the weather, unforeseen disasters and events.

These uncertainties and possibilities are areas we need protection from and choices such as insurance policies in case of disasters, medical emergencies, accidents, fire and theft can give you peace of mind.

Making appointments with your physician and dentist for regular check-ups to prevent major health issues and to choose a safe neighborhood to raise your children in are also good decisions.

These are proven methods to protect us and to take the pressure off when things go wrong.

At the end of the day – we create our own reality by planning for the future, inviting people into our lives and interacting with situations and challenges we have either created or supported along the way.

You can choose – to win or to lose.

UNLEASHING THE BEAST OF VIRAL VIDEO
TO FIGHT ANIMAL ABUSE:
HOW I USED MY VIDEO MARKETING SUPER POWERS TO DO GOOD

DAVID B. WRIGHT

I love animals. I have had dogs and cats most of my life and we currently have four dogs, one of whom was a stray who we rescued in the mountains in June. She was severely underweight, had 15 ticks on her, and had probably never had her shots. You could easily count eight ribs just looking at her side. We brought her home, got her checked out by the vet, got her up to date on her shots and so on. A few weeks later, we found out she was pregnant! The vet said she could have anywhere from six to twelve puppies and sure enough, she went big and ended up having TWELVE puppies! My wife, Heather, and I call her the gift that keeps on giving! We found homes for all of the puppies, and are keeping one of them. All of them lived and are healthy and happy in their new homes.

More recently, Heather was looking at her Facebook feed and sees this video that someone here in Atlanta had posted on his Facebook page, showing him intentionally setting off fireworks behind his dog. The video showed him looking at the dog before going inside, closing the door behind him and leaving the dog out there alone with the fireworks, while his 13-year-old daughter was filming the whole thing, and you could hear her laughing at the end of the video. I was standing there in shock.

I couldn't just not do something.

I'm a marketer, best-selling author, and run a company called W3 Group Marketing. We help businesses attract more clients, primarily via online marketing strategies. We've been in business helping clients for over ten years.

I do a lot of video marketing and video SEO, and over 94% of my last 80 videos have reached page one of Google for our target keyword in less than one hour. I felt compelled to use my super power to get the word out and make this story go big so hopefully this kind of prank wouldn't happen again, to this dog or others.

I got a copy of the video, created a new YouTube account, uploaded the video, worked some of my magic, and shared it with social media and the news media. Reporters were calling me trying to find people to interview for the story. It got news coverage the very next day on several of the local news stations – Channel 2, Channel 5, Channel 11, Channel 46 plus CNN, and started to take on a life of its own. It got picked up by Associated Press and was distributed to, and aired by, news stations across the country and around the world – including Hong Kong, Australia and South Korea. It was even on People, Mundo Hispanico and Inside Edition.

It went absolutely crazy on social media. I also shared it with a few pet lovers groups and rescue organizations. Within a matter of days, there were over 73,000 comments, more than 90,000 reactions on social media (likes, angry, sad, etc. – obviously almost all of these were angry and sad reactions), and over 109,000 shares.

On Channel 2's website alone, it got over 6.2 Million views. I've counted these, documented, and verified with screen shots.

There's even more: I've been able to count about 12 million views. Yes, that's in less than one week.

Many sites don't show a view count, so we estimated further views based on Nielsen ratings, live TV broadcast reach, market share statistics, publicly available website traffic estimates and so on. This video very likely got well over 50 million views, perhaps even over 100 million views within just one week – and all because some guy abused a defenseless dog and not only posted it on social media but defended his actions there too.

The individual was charged with animal cruelty and was fined the maximum fine allowable by law. That story was covered on the news as well. But perhaps more importantly, he's been tried in the court of public opinion. He'll certainly think twice before abusing an animal again, we can hope.

Lessons learned and what this means to you:

One little thing can lead to huge results. But you have to take action and set that wheel in motion.

Emotions – Emotionally charged issues get shared more than those that don't tap in to your emotions. Naturally, in most cases you don't want to disgust your audience so the type of video this is wouldn't help your public perception, but having an emotional tie-in can be extremely powerful. Remember the McDonald's commercial with the baby swinging and smiling from the Super Bowl a few years back? That got shared so much outside of the times McDonald's paid to have it air, that they ended up with quite a reach. People adored it because it was cute and made them feel good.

Principles – If you don't stand for something, you don't stand for anything. I'm firmly against animal abuse and if I hadn't taken action on this, the individual might have gotten off scot-free, and might have even done it again to that poor dog. It also might not have served as such a powerful example of what not to do. Take a stand, put it out there and don't let a fear of negative consequences keep you from doing what's right.

Leverage Urgency and Competition – One news station was planning to air the story the following day. Then another station decided to air it that night, so the first station moved it up in the schedule so they didn't get scooped. Playing one powerful tool against another can get faster results, and a multiplier effect, than playing solo.

Alliances & Cause Supporters – large groups of people with similar interests, or who stand strongly for or against something related, can be leveraged to help get a broader reach quickly. The ALS Ice Bucket Challenge from a couple of years ago, as silly as it might have seemed, raised $220 Million in donations. That money has allowed scientists to isolate the gene that causes the disease, and make great leaps toward finding a cure.

Follow up – if there's a reason for a second part to the story, such as this individual's court case, it can get even more traction. Many of the stations aired part of his trial and the circus around it as a follow up story. PETA even had people there at the courthouse protesting what he'd done.

Everyone does something well. How can you use your superpower for good?

INSPIRATION

PAT SLATTERY

When I look back at some of my earliest memories I think about what has driven me to overcome any obstacle and where I have found inspiration to keep going despite circumstances

Here I will share some of my story so you may find inspiration that will also allow you to keep going despite circumstances

As a young boy, I was not used to having very much in terms of material goods or even at times extra food, I certainly did not have many treats, I had an amazing Mum and Dad whom I truly believe done their best for me and my brothers and sisters, in particular my Mum, what an inspiration she was to me, even though at the time I did not realise it

My mum received a pension payment from my Dads pension of just £70 per week for which she had to use to feed, clothe a large family and then also manage household bills

As a young woman, my mum married my dad who had previously been married and whose wife passed away and leaving him with 9 children, this did not deter my mum, so at 24years his junior my mum married and took on the role of supporting him and raising his children, she then went on to give birth to 7 of her own children so extending family of 9 to 16.

The importance of knowing this is so that it will give you a better understanding of how incredible this woman was then and still is today, So as you can imagine by the time I had come along to join this already large family, money and material goods were few and far between, however my amazing mum always managed to find a way to make sure that we always had enough, I have memories of my mum walking 4 miles from our home to the largest supermarket and coming home with up to 8 full shopping bags full of supplies, this she done because it meant her money would stretch further and she could make sure that everyone in our home had enough so we never went hungry. This showed me that once you have a desire to do something and that if the desire is strong enough you will do whatever it takes to make sure it happens. My mum had a very strong desire to take care of her family. This is just one of many stories I could share with you about my mum

I have early memories of going to our local shop to collect empty cardboard boxes so I could cut the shape of my shoes out on them so I could put it inside my shoes to stop the water from coming through the holes in the soles of my shoes

Moving forward a few years, at 14 years old I took a job working in a hotel in the city, first I was hired as a dishwasher and shortly after I was given the job as porter or concierge as it is now better known, this meant the world to me, having this job meant that I would have some money that I could buy nice things with and allow me to bring some money home to help my mum

I kept this job and did not go back to school anymore so I was now very quickly gone from a boy to a man. A year later I left this job and began working as a doorman in a nightclub at weekends, I took a job delivering newspapers during the afternoons Monday to Friday, in the morning I worked in the printing office of the newspaper company, on midweek evenings I worked as a doorman in a fast-food restaurant, I took a job as a security officer in a menswear store on Saturdays, I became a workaholic

I discovered I had a desire to make money so I took any job I could fit in so I could make more money

Eventually I went from working as a doorman to creating a very large security company that in its lifetime generated over Twenty-Five Million Euro for me, I have since had multiple companies that have generated millions of euros for both me and my partners. I have developed strategies for hundreds of companies and individuals to generate both extra income in their businesses and extra time in their lives

So let me share where I got the inspiration to do this and how it became possible

It took me many years to discover how this happened for me but when I look back on my life I can see where some of this drive and determination came from.

I had many inspiring people in my life and sometimes without even knowing it they were guiding me in the right direction, there are way too many stories to go into on this to fit into this short story

What I discovered that I consider was my driving force was a message I came across from the great Jim Rohn many years ago. Here I will share it with you

What have you had enough of?

Once you have decided you have had enough this will change your life dramatically, when I say had enough I mean it in a way that you feel it in every cell in your body that you truly believe that you have had enough of something that no longer serves you or may never have served you at any point of your life

For me I guess I had enough of not having enough, I had enough of watching my mum struggle, I had enough of not having enough week left at the end of my pay check, I had enough of walking around a store checking the price of products at the same time checking how much money I had in my pocket to make sure I could afford what I wanted

These are just some of the things that I had enough of, ask yourself this, what do you have enough of, what is it that you no longer want in your life?

When I decided that I was going to own business I shared this goal with some people who thought it was a silly idea, people like me don't own businesses, they thought it was funny the idea that someone of my background would consider owning a business, and for a while I believed them too

Until one day I decided I had enough of playing small, I had enough of people telling me where I belonged and that I could not achieve whatever I put my mind to achieving "I decided I had enough" and then I committed to an act that said "I have had enough"

You must commit to an act that says "I have had enough "

The next step was decision

Decisions can be really emotional, this is what gives you the knot in your stomach, knowing that you want to decide to do the action that you need to do in order to get you closer to your desired result.

In Order to make progress you must decide. Commit to the decision to take the action that will bring you wherever it is you desire to be

The next thing I discovered was Desire

When you discover what, you have had enough of and you create the desire to change and you really feel this desire then you start the journey of achieving all that you want in life and business

Desire is that feeling you get in your gut that tells you whatever you are thinking of doing is truly possible, it is the feeling of knowing that you will do whatever it takes to make it happen, that you will commit to this desire and believe in yourself that you can be do have anything in life that you want to have. It tells you that even though you may not know the way right now that you will find the way, you will do whatever it takes to learn the skills, put in the work do whatever is required of you to achieve whatever it is you truly desire. I discovered a real desire to grow

Desire can be triggered by many different things, it may be something you read in this book, it may be something someone says to you or something you have seen, desire comes from inside and cannot be gotten from an outside source. You must feel it within you

The next thing I discovered was RESOLVE

The Definition of resolve – Promising yourself that you will never give up! Two of the most powerful words you can tell yourself "I Will"

What is your "I Will" statement? You must tell yourself what you will have, not what you hope to have, be very clear on what you will have!

When you create your "I Will" statement you are now making a statement of intent

This I discovered was a tremendous tool in helping me focus on my goals. When you create your "I Will" statement you are setting your intention, once you set your intention

Pay ATTENTION to your INTENTION

This means that you find out what you have had enough of, decide to commit to an action that says "I have had enough", find the desire inside you to go after whatever it is that you desire in life then set your intention and DO whatever it takes to get there.

"If it is easy, do it easy, if it is hard do it hard, just get it done"

These tools are what have served me so well in life, these tools have helped me overcome many challenges in both my life and business and I am sure they will help you too.

Take this information and apply it!

MANY OF MY EVERYDAY HEROES
ARE ALSO CLIENTS!

GARY KISSEL

Whatever level of success that I have achieved is the result of being of service to others. My motto is *"I amplify your greatness"* and my mission is to build long-lasting relationships for mutually-beneficial results.

In my efforts to help professionals build and grow their businesses, I have encountered many clients that I classify as *"everyday heroes"*. In the following paragraphs I will introduce four individuals to you who are some of my favorites and will explain why I think they qualify as a hero.

In general, a hero is a person that lifts others up. *Givers* take this course of action with the inner understanding that when people are given a *hand up* a ripple effect is created. Most *recipients* will remember profoundly that they were given help at some stage and in turn will want to do the same for others.

I'm sure that you have experienced a sense of fulfillment when you have given a *hand up*.

With that said, my first hero is Ralph. Ralph is 74 and has vast experience as a mortgage industry coach. Ralph's most famous principle is *"1% more each day"* (I wear it on my wrist). He is passionate about coaching others to greater success--and his golf game.

I started working with Ralph over a year ago and he is the kind of student that everyone hopes to teach. He listens and applies. That is, he puts into action the lessons that he is taught. He is exceptional because of his laser-like focus which he directs towards reaching his goals (or improving his golf handicap).

Ralph had just over 500 connections on LinkedIn when we started working together, but today he has over 13,000!

This number is more impressive when it's revealed that he sought to focus on mortgage industry contacts---not just a random scattering of acquaintances. He has told me that ninety percent of his new clients have come from his efforts on LinkedIn.

There is no stopping Ralph! Despite suffering a heart attack (and pacemaker surgery) last month, Ralph was quickly back in the office a few days later. He was working on his webinar presentation and sharing his coaching genius with prospective clients.

Ralph has adopted an internet persona as well, look for "The Mortgage Godfather." He recorded a testimonial for me and it can be found on YouTube at https://www.youtube.com/watch?v=IhofgVkP75Y. Take a look. You will enjoy his no-nonsense approach.

Another hero client of mine is named Tina. She is an exceptional photographer and nature lover. One thing that she is not is a *techie*. Tina wasn't the easiest to work with for this reason.

Optimizing her LinkedIn profile wasn't her idea of a good time. We did persevere however, over several sessions. She finally crafted a pretty impressive presence on LinkedIn but over the course of our time together, Tina developed a new love. She became a Periscope influencer. She loved to broadcast her activities far and wide and now she's quite prominent on that platform.

This all began to change a bit when a few months ago I got an email from Tina. She wanted to know if what she had received from LinkedIn was legit or not. I checked it out and informed her that she had in fact, been selected as a LinkedIn Profinder! Profinder was a beta test program at the time. Tina was chosen, LinkedIn said, because of "her impressive profile".

Professionals chosen for this innovative program launch were *vetted* by LinkedIn. Those approved would be suggested (by LinkedIn) as a recommended professional in a certain area of expertise to someone searching LinkedIn for help or training in that given field. In general, it was designed as a lead-generating experiment and it still continues on today. (I was recently honored to be selected as a "marketing consultant" under this program.)

Tina is passionate about and committed to capturing the best head shot of her subject and she speaks often to groups about the value of having a great photo. When she is not helping others in this fashion she is in her backyard releasing butterflies that she has raised or is out completing another pet rescue. Tina lives a life of service and enjoys it immensely.

Another hero of mine is Jeffrey Combs. Like me, he is from the Midwest and his consulting organization is called Golden Mastermind Seminars, Inc.

He lectures around the country on how procrastination and inaction kills many business endeavors. Jeffrey helps small business owners become better sales people by teaching them how to become "master listeners". I have heard him talk about how many people simply strive to "slide safely into their grave" while few dare to take the risk to become great.

Jeffrey is known for his keen ability to *read* people and he hosts a free national podcast weekly. Jeffrey has a continual flow of new clients because of the highly-valued content that he gives away. His in-person seminars are just $20 a head. From his seminars and his follow up efforts, he has enrolled many into his coaching packages. He is another one with a laser-like focus.

My next hero is a client, but our relationship goes far beyond the norm. My daughter considers herself a *digital nomad* and a *global citizen*. She just completed a four continent tour after experiencing a spiritual awakening in Peru. I am no doubt learning more from her than she is from me.

While she loved kite surfing off the Pacific coast of Ecuador, she felt called to team up with a partner and immerse herself in the Syrian refugee crisis. Off to Greece she went to take video documentation of the actual struggles encountered by these tens of thousands who still are literally without a country or a home. Syria was too dangerous to return to and most European countries have pushed them back from their borders.

One video that she published on Face Book showed the majority at one camp to be mostly women, children and elderly folks. A tent school was prominent as were the children's drawings from a trauma therapy class. Because her travel partner was from Belgium, he and my daughter were extended sympathies from some of the refugees in the wake of the terrorist attacks that occurred at the Brussels airport and Metro station last March.

Think about that for a minute. Refugees without a home and without knowledge of where they might be from day to day extended empathy to complete strangers that happened to have a homeland under attack. I wonder if these refugees knew that in Belgium there has been a growing sentiment to not "feed the refugees" and some have even called for a Guantanamo Bay style camp to house them. Regardless, that moment at the camp was a profoundly memorable one for my daughter and her partner. Rewards like this are commonly realized when we indulge ourselves fully in a service-giving life style.

Heroes are all around us. The real question isn't what are they doing but instead, what are each of us are doing day in and day out to better the lives of others.. Are you a hero to anyone? Am I? "If we truly live a life of service to one another, then it is likely that others will respect and admire our choice to live our lives in a distinguished way"

Lastly, I salute YOU as a hero for living your life to lift up others into more opportunity and hope. As always, I wish you phenomenal success into the future!

SUIT UP, SHOW UP AND DO THE NEXT INDICATED STEP

KATHLEEN GAGE

Spring of 2009 was shaping up to be very exciting. I had made a decision to participate in a marathon as a gift to myself for my 55th birthday. Having packed on a few excess pounds due to "the good life," this was an opportunity for me to get in shape as well as do something good for others.

Excited about the prospects of crossing the finish line the weekend of the Portland Marathon in October of the same year, I threw myself into the training offered by Team in Training.

True to my nature, I poured my heart and soul into the training. I loved the feeling of pushing myself in this way.

I was participating as a power walker rather than a runner. Three months into my training, I had dropped 40 pounds, I was getting in fabulous shape and felt great. I was on top of the world.

Hitting Potholes

All came to a screeching halt at mile eight of a training day when my right foot hit a pothole. I felt an incredibly sharp pain accompanied by a snapping sound. I immediately knew my ankle was broken.

My greatest frustration was knowing that I couldn't give my dad the gift I had planned; a trip for he and my mom to enjoy Portland for the marathon and celebrate his 82nd birthday.

My mom and dad were actually okay with the change in plans. Mostly because my father had been slowing way down physically and now he could stay close to home.

Within days of my accident, my father was diagnosed with small cell lung cancer and multiple brain lesions.

Time Limits Are Real

Although the oncologist told the family my dad may have a year or two, within a matter of weeks, my father passed on. Ironically, he passed the day he and my mom would have been returning from Portland for the marathon. I believe my broken ankle had all been part of the divine plan to be fully present for my father.

The loss to my sisters and I was nothing compared to the deep heartbreak my mother was going through having been married to my father for nearly 61 years.

With no way of knowing what was coming next, I dutifully answered a personal calling to be available for my mother's care. For the next two years I drove to and from my home to my mother's home and hospital bedside countless times. I knew the 400-mile drive extremely well.

Loss Continues

Shortly after my mother's passing, several of our rescue animals passed on. Bucky our goat, Aries our Boxer and Storm, our tortoise cat, all lived to a ripe old age before taking their final journey over the rainbow bridge.

There were times I wondered if I would have the energy to keep up with all that was occurring. Yet, each day I would get up and do what was in front of me. Many times, I didn't have the time or energy to do much else.

What I learned to do was suit up, show up and do the next indicated step while continually asking for the guidance and strength to get through another day. I had the deepest understanding of what it means to serve others at the deepest level possible.

Hindsight is 20/20

Looking back over the years of uncertainty and great loss, I am incredibly grateful for the depth of knowledge I gained from each and every experience. Knowledge that has enhanced all levels of my life. Knowledge and experience that I share with my clients to help them through tough times while continuing to run their businesses. Knowledge and experience that lets me know I cannot take one minute of one day for granted.

Knowledge and experience that gives me a passion for every day to live fully, love deeply and appreciation sincerely.

I am in awe that, in spite of my life feeling completely upside down during my dad's passing, my mom's illness and passing and the loss of so many fur babies, there was (and is) a deep level of serenity I experienced when I simply trusted the process.

I am also in awe of the fact my business never floundered. In fact, it grew. I truly believe I was given the right ideas at just the right time to adjust how my business was structured. This allowed me to fully serve my market while taking care of family needs.

I suppose when I was my most vulnerable I was also my most teachable and receptive. This I know to be true; life takes on very deep meaning and joy when we surrender to why we are here.

I would be remiss not to share a bit about how it was possible for me to take so much time to be there for family. The most important reason is because I knew this was what I was meant to do.

I never asked, "Why is this happening to me." Rather I would give thanks that I was able to be present for what was occurring.

Secondly, my business afforded me the opportunity to do the things that were most important.

However, it wasn't just having the business that allowed this opportunity. Had I not trusted the guidance I received to structure things the way I did likely would have turned out very differently.

Our Business as a Vehicle

The fact is; our businesses are simply a vehicle to touch the lives of those we are meant to. This happens on many levels.

We impact our customers and clients by providing them with products and services to improve their personal and professional lives. We provide for our families in a way they have comfort and safety. We provide for our communities through the donations we make and the time we offer in service. We provide for our animals a life they likely take for granted.

To this day, I still pray the prayer of St. Francis, "Lord, make me an instrument." My greatest hope is that I answer the calling, whatever it may be.

GIVE PEOPLE AN OPPORTUNITY

PHIL PERRIN

This is a story about a team training in statistical process control and the changes they made when given an opportunity to make a difference.

During the feedback session at the end of their training course, I asked the class what they thought of the course and how they wanted to apply it in their day jobs. One of the guys, Steve, replied, "the course was great! There are several improvements we could make but unfortunately, our manager won't give us the opportunity to apply it", the others agreed. Who's your manager? Curt they said so I offered to talk with him on their behalf.

Later that afternoon I met with Curt and explained that the students wanted make savings by applying the knowledge and techniques learnt on the course. How much time will they need he asked? How about an hour a week? An hour a week for 6 people that's 24 hour's production I will lose a month! he exclaimed. But what if they can save that time? OK he said I am a fair man, they can try for a month and if you can help them, save more time than they spend, they can continue to do it, if not we will stop it. Sounds fair, we will start in the morning.

The next day the team were asked to meet up in the production meeting room. I explained what Curt had said and asked them where they wanted to start. Steve said we have loads of issues that we spend time on, where do we start?

Suggest you just brainstorm the issues you are seeing first for a few minutes. The team came up with the following issues, captured on a flipchart:

Incorrect Drawings; Tight Tolerances; Missing Dimensions; Wrong Materials; Wrong Parts; Tooling; Broken Fixtures; Worn Machine; Calibration; Snapped Tap; Blunt Drill and Work Instructions.

Great we have 12 in total we now need to prioritize these, to say six, we can do this by giving everyone 3 votes and the six with the highest votes win.

The prioritized issues were: Incorrect Drawings, Tight Tolerances, Wrong Materials, Snapped Tap, Calibration and Work Instructions.

How are you going to measure these? Suggest you keep it simple for now.

We can use a simple tally chart and tick how many times each problem occurs each day said Bernie. But what about cost I asked, how are you going to track that? We could just record how long we spend on the problem say one tick for fifteen minutes said Tony.

The rest of the team agreed to collect the data for a week and reconvene the following Friday.

The next week Phil collected the data sheets before the meeting and created two Pareto charts from the totals on the Tally sheets. The team arrived enthusiastic to see the results.

This is your baseline of the current issues the stake in the ground to quantify any improvements you make, over time. The Issues Pareto chart indicated the most frequent in descending order of occurrences were due to Incorrect Work Instructions, Broken Taps, Incorrect Drawings and Tight Tolerances.

However, the highest time spent on the problem was on Tight Tolerances.

WOW said Bernie every time this tight tolerance occurs, we spend about 3 hours trying to machine it. Can anyone explain what this tight tolerance is? Yes, said Dave, it's just a countersink on the top of a hole that guides a locating pin into a hole aligning two parts. What is the tolerance? Its plus or minus half a thou concentric to the centre of the hole and has a zero bottom tolerance and half a thou top tolerance on depth. It takes ages to manually get this right on a milling machine.

Does it need to be that tight? No not really said Dave but, we have to work to the drawings, as this is a safety critical part. Have you spoken with the design office about this Dave? No! we are not allowed Dave replied. OK how many of these parts do you need to manufacture? About 200 more. OK so that's 200 x 3 hours = 600 hours you could potentially save.

What about the work instruction errors? We have already highlighted those for correction on Monday said Tony there were a few incorrect part number typos and missed operations.

OK we need to get this tight tolerance changed are you free to come up to see the designer with me Dave. Yes, Dave replied. Right well done, can the rest of the team collect the data for another week?

In the design office, the designer was sitting at his desk so we asked him if there was any possibility of opening up the tolerance. He looked at the drawing and agreed the tolerance was too tight. That looks like the default tolerance on the CAD system has been applied and it should have been larger.

How much can you open the tolerance up? Dave asked. How does 20 thou concentric to the hole and 20 thou on the upper limit of the depth sound. Sounds great, said Dave, we would not need to use the machine for that we could just use an air drill with a countersink bit. How long would that take to machine now? About 30 Seconds he replied.

How long will it take to raise a change request? Can do it now the engineer replied, if you get the approvals signed and you can start to use the new process today, as that dimension is not critical to the fit form or function of the part. I will also open up the default tolerance to 10 thou.

Great there you go Dave, one simple question and you have saved 600 hours. The engineer raised a Change Request and it was approved by the end of the day.

That was amazing said Dave that should convince Curt that its worth giving us some time to improve and it will sure make my work less stressful.

The next Friday meeting everyone was excited as Dave had told them what had happened with the designer. Phil put the two Pareto charts on the wall, the tight tolerance issue had disappeared with Work instructions now the smallest issue and broken Taps being the largest on both charts.

Congratulations team you have already saved over 600 hours and there is still more to go after.

There's more said Jim on the broken taps, I measured how many times we used them before they broke and they always broke after 30 uses, we now only use them 28 times and throw them away and have not seen a breakage since.

Curt joined the meeting at this point to see how we were doing and let the team walk him through what they had achieved. He was so impressed that he took the whole team out for a drink to show his gratitude, since then the team have made significant improvements with measurable savings, all because they were given an opportunity.

I am a firm believer that nobody goes to work to do a bad job and if given the opportunity to improve they will.

THE PLANTING OF THE SEED

ROSANNE D'AUSILIO

My name is Rosanne D'Ausilio. I was born and grew up in Cleveland, Ohio, but at age 23 I moved to New York City. My parents who then moved to Florida were conservative, frugal and careful. I was hardwired to grow up, get married, have a couple of kids, and be a stay at home mom. Well I'm happy to say it didn't turn out that way.

Ultimately I was divorced with 2 young children and worked (for someone else) to support them and pay the mortgage. As luck (or fate) would have it, 20 years ago I visited a friend who had a house in the Dominican Republic on the North Coast. I was only there for a long weekend but I fell in love with the country, the people (warm and heart centered), the weather, the beach, the mountains, the food, all of it. I wanted what she had but was it possible? Up until that time it wasn't even something I had ever thought about. In retrospect, this was a defining moment in my life.

I took a risk (outrageous for me with my upbringing, especially in a foreign country) and I bought land there. Every 2 years I visited for 1 week – that was my vacation in those days. I always stayed in All Inclusives and put one day aside to visit the land. This purchase was the seed that set in motion my pull to return, my future, my pipedream of living in paradise although I certainly didn't know it then.

Subsequently, I had an opportunity to go back to school and get a Masters and a PhD which earned me the title of Industrial Psychologist (knowing what makes companies tick) which gave me the impetus to start my own business. I love working with people. My bias was and is on the people side so I specialized in the contact center industry, spoke at conferences (my way of doing sales), consulted, coached, created customized customer service skills training, and wrote a number of books (14) on the topic, establishing myself as a customer service expert.

I yearned for independence, both professionally and financially and hated the winters when I could never get warm. So I took one of Matt Bacak's first workshops. There were 6 or 8 of us there. Just the number that would fit around his conference table. In that hands-on workshop I bought a domain for a tips newsletter called How to Kick Your Customer Service Up a Notch (www.HumanTechtips.com) That ramped up from zero to 17000 subscribers in about a year, and has over 500 tips and is still active today.

Another important skill I learned was how to write and submit articles. Within 30 days of posting one article, I made $15000 in consulting fees from a company in Chicago who read it. I continue to write articles and books, and consistently up my credibility. These endeavors allow me to raise my fees, and for those who like credentials, I am very well credentialed.

When the market began going downhill, the first thing to go were trainings. So I focused on consulting and coaching. It turns out this is one of my favorite things to do and I do it well. I have laser focus when working with clients. I can easily see obstacles in the way of their goals, what challenges they are facing--real and imagined--and what actions *can be taken/ need to be taken* right now or '*by when.*' We also uncover limited belief systems that hold people back from being their best self. My experience helps people see what's possible for them to fulfill their dreams. After all, I am no different than you.

Measurable results show up for my clients. One client realized $70,000 in revenue when I coached her to charge for what she was giving away for free! At present I am currently on retainer on a 2 year contract providing coaching for a company's CEO. When we do middle management, we provide a SOW (Statement of Work) with a beginning and an end (usually 10 sessions) in order to get approval. This isn't required with CEO's. For them, they understand coaching is an ongoing process, not an event. Back to my dream. Almost eighteen years passed and I had done nothing with the land. I had architectural drawings for a 3 bedroom, 2 bath house with a kidney shaped pool in the back but never followed through. When I was in the Dominican Republic 10 years ago April I said to myself, "That's it, let's go see some furnished condos."

While there I purchased a small one bedroom in the hills, 5 minutes from town. Very quiet environment, the afternoon Trade Winds blew gently through the window, the place was bright and airy and I loved it. I have a visceral memory of the curtain slapping me in the face as the wind picked up. That's what sold me right then and there. I bought it with the logical intention of having a place to stay whenever I vacationed in the Dominican Republic.

For about 2 years it was rented for 2-3 months at a time. I would vacation there for 2 weeks, then 3 weeks, and then a month. Now the planted seed is being watered (in retrospect of course). I began to see what's possible and if I could make this work.

Of course there were obstacles/learning experiences. When I visited for 3 months, I was not quite sure I had enough money to last that length of time. Unfortunately, the power went out and in order for me to be in business I absolutely need internet and phone. I made the necessary investments to keep me in business. I purchased an inverter (a battery back-up system) so that I have seamless power whenever there's an outage.

The other difficulty I experienced was the inconvenience (and stress) of packing up the apartment in order to rent it again. Ultimately decided to no longer rent and come and stay myself for longer periods of time. I would stay for 4 months. Then it became 5, and now I'm in the Dominican Republic half of the year. The seeds are now germinating.

In order to make this arrangement work for 6 months, I must have reliable internet first and foremost. Therefore, I have the best connection money can buy.

Second, I have a Magic Jack (an internet phone that allows me to make/receive calls to/ from the US and Canada for a yearly fee). I chose my New York area code so unless you heard roosters in the background, you don't know where you were reaching me. I use my Magic Jack on my computer as well as the app on my phone with good service in the US, Canada, Europe, and of course, the Caribbean.

I was recently interviewed and I noticed the caller's area code was 203 and I remarked, "Oh you're in Connecticut?" He said, "No I'm in British Columbia, the publication is in Connecticut. And I see you're in NY." I said, "No I'm in the Dominican Republic!" We had a nice laugh and again I felt like I was watering the seeds.

There are some days I work 8-10 hours and wonder what's different? The difference is I look out my window and see palm trees swaying while I'm working in shorts and a tee shirt. I'm not in a bleak office in New York chilled to the bone, bundled up, seeing snow/ slush, and traffic out my window.

So long as I give good service--which I am known for--no one cares what my zip code is. I am no longer tied down geographically and it feels great. The seeds are beginning to flower.

I schedule my coaching calls, appointments, and consulting in the mornings so I have the afternoons to either work or play. I consider myself semi retired but if I'm not playing tennis, going to Zumba (Latin Dance) classes, or under an umbrella at the beach, I am working. I love what I do!

I feel like I live 2 lives. In the States I have all my creature comforts, a lovely home with central air, an attached garage that houses my new (to me) BMW Black Convertible (2002), and all the shops, grocery stores, libraries, restaurants, etc. at my fingertips.

In the Dominican Republic I have no air conditioning and no car, neither of which I need. I use moto Conchos which are motorbike taxis. I hire one by the week to take me to/from the gym or town.

To me, my life in the Dominican Republic represents peace and serenity. I lead a simple life there. I feel spiritually fit, grounded, and my most authentic self. Clearly I created this lifestyle for myself…my piece of Paradise.

I don't worry about money any more. I believe there is abundance in the world and I feel confident it's not just for everyone else. It's also for me. When I find a coin on the ground, I pick it up and say, 'thank you, thank you, thank you.' I believe it represents abundance; a reminder that I have abundance in my life.

I am now on solid ground and say yes to life!!! As Wayne Dyer is famous for saying, 'when you believe it, you'll see it.'

My seeds are continually being watered and I now imagine a small tree growing with beautiful red flowers, leaves fluttering gently to the ground, representing my incredible lifestyle in Paradise.

I LOVE HAVING MY OWN BUSINESS

SUZANNE EDWARDS

Some people love doing it, some have never tried, you might be doing it right now or thinking about doing it, others might put you of; so, what are you waiting for; just do it!

Children are unique and not all children learn in a large classroom in the same way. The challenges faced with my children is that from a really young age, they were ready to read. At the time the web was not prolific with access to information as it is today. I used to go up to their school complaining about the level of teaching not being high enough. I had meetings with the Head teacher. She fully supported the teachers in what they had to achieve. I knew if I did nothing about it, then my children would not learn in a way I would like them to learn. You can visualise what could happen if I did nothing and if you are a parent you know how painful it is when you really want to help your child to make them the very best they can be at school so when they grow up their journey of life is not hard. Both my son and daughter have an entrepreneurial spirit and one which both my husband and I have nurtured in them from a young age. We taught them from young that they are not followers, but leaders. Everything they now do in life is about them taking the lead, overcoming challenges and making a difference.

Dissatisfied with the schooling my children were receiving, I felt it was up to me to help both my children in the best possible way. We had the option of moving our children from one school to another with the view that there was no guarantee the next school would be better and they wanted to stay so they could be with their friends. This is a key factor when a child is so young as having close school friends, helps them to learn about socialising and contributes towards building their personality. I therefore decided to keep them at the same school and thought about how I could help them outside of school. Other parents could relate to my situation which was interesting.

Noting the missing gap, I quickly set up my business to help support parents and others who can see their child is ready to learn beyond the school curriculum. Parents who were advised by their child's school, that much of the learning is based around social skills or they did not teach those topics to the children at such a young age, decided to join us, to help make a difference for their child.

With huge support from my husband, I set up Little Big Leaders to help other parents who wanted their child to start leaning from a young age and cover more complex topics enabling them to be at least two years ahead academically. We provide fun learning for child from the age of 3½ to 11 years. Believe you me, children can read and write from a very young age, as we have taught many who have gone onto some of the top private schools. We had one student, let's call her Sandy, who joined us last year who could not speak English and once she finished our Reading and Maths programme, she gained entry to a private school. This is just within a year. When her father originally enquired, he did not believe it would be possible for her to learn to read; once she completed the first lesson; he was hooked. As she progressed on the Reading Programme, he advised, when he dropped his daughter of at the centre each week, he and his wife would go to the church at the top of the road and say a pray for me. Time after time, we hear these real-life situations, where our lessons help so many children who at first where told by their school, that their child is struggling or at the bottom of the class. When they join us at Little Big Leaders, attend regular and complete their homework, many go onto being the top of the class and gaining entry to some of the most prestigious schools in London. We are fortunate when we run our Summer School, as many people fly in from different parts of the world, as many advise we have an excellent track record, professional tutors and a great environment. We really aim to add fun for the children who enjoy attending and many know they are doing well as they tell us, when they, receive a gold star or trophy for outstanding work at school – this is really amazing.

Many mums come to us in tears when they repeat the sad things the teacher advised about their child and when that same child stays with us for years, often there are tears when the mother updates, advising her child gained entry to a top private school – those tears, are tears, of joy.

Providing a "service" business is special as you are creating something where there is either a missing gap or you want to improve upon something. These are the elements I looked at doing, that is, helping children from the age of 3½ to read and write as well as help children from the age of 5 improve in their Maths and English. Creating a product that can do this is remarkable. You see what is missing and you create something from nothing which can really make the difference. This business is about me believing children can learn from a really young age. It is about understanding about the skills of leadership and how this can be instilled in a young child through structure. It is about understanding that not all children learn in large groups and not all children will eventually work for someone else.

When you set up your own business, it is about taking a real passion, turning it into a huge success and being smart enough to do it quickly. You must keep going as there will be times you will be working on your own through the early hours. You must always know that you are making a difference to those who buy your products, especially those who stay with you for years. This is the thing many entrepreneurs forget, it is easy to set up a business, but one of the hardest things is to sustain the momentum when the times get tough as there will be tough times but you have to really rise above those. Remember what you are doing is making a difference. When it makes a difference to one of your clients, they will inform a family member or friend and then the cycle continues. Business for me is about strength of character, having faith in yourself and courage to do it.

As you start your journey of greatness in setting up your own business, you too will have people who want to work with you, because you are different. It is about having the right people around you making your business successful. You took the initial step of wanting to change something or create a product or help others in your own special way. I hope by you reading this chapter you feel inspired to also make a difference in the lives of others as this is what you are really doing, when setting up your own business.

Surround yourself with like-minded positive people who will offer guidance and time for you when you can bounce ideas of each other. Sometimes it is your clients who come up with some really great ideas where you can improve on different areas of your business and some you may be able to implement straight away, while others may need more strategic planning. Also, refer back to your initial notes on what you plan to do and I would say one of the most important things to do is to focus on what you want to do. Take advise from the right people. Even better if you can speak to those in a similar industry or running their own business longer then yourself who could offer suggestions, then listen and take on board what is suggested.

Many of my clients have been with me for years offering business suggestions without even realising it, as these are often part of a deep conversation we might be having rather than me asking what are the areas you feel we should improve upon. Sometimes you need to listen beyond what a client tells you.

I sincerely love having my own business, the people who work for me and clients who have been with me for years, as well as, the new ones joining shortly. It is really rewarding at so many different levels, that is, from the day to day, to the long-term vision. You must have a vision so you and your team have something to aspire towards achieving, so when you are up late working through the night you know in your heart it was worthwhile. I wish you huge success and remember not everyone is doing it – I hope you are?

HOW TO FIND MEANING IN YOUR WORK

SHARVIN EXUBRIO

More and more money. That's the main objective of a business, I thought. As I planted myself in one seminar after another, exploring various ways to be successful, I noticed there was a common theme among successful people. They were incredible marketers. They were incredible at marketing their image. They were incredible at marketing their business. And they were incredible at marketing their vision. I realized if I were to ever be successful, I had to learn how to be an incredible marketer too.

With that in mind, I decided to invest all my savings into courses and programs that could mold me into the marketing wizard I wanted to be. After six months of learning, I realized just how little I knew and how much more there was to know. Six more months of practicing and I realized the skills I picked up could be applied in my everyday life too. Another six months in and I realized how creativity and inspiration could come from even the smallest of things. I was getting better and better as the months progressed and I was not about to stop.

As a student, I was constantly told to trust the process and to simply follow the steps laid out. And for a while, that proved to be the optimal move. I was steadily building a list of subscribers online and by marketing various products via email, I was able to make a comfortable living. I thought if I could continue doing the exact same thing, I would eventually scale it into a multi-million dollar business just like my mentors. But I was wrong.

Following the same standard operating procedure for 2 years proved to me that if I'm not constantly improving and moving forward, I'm moving backward. My subscriber list was growing bigger and bigger but my engagement rate was going lower and lower. It came to a point where an email to my 21849 subscribers may not even get one sale. It was then that I knew something had to be corrected and it had to be corrected fast.

I approached a couple of my teachers to gain some clarity on what wasn't working. Some of them pointed out ways to refine my landing page and product funnel. Some of them offered advice on traffic sources. One of them even gave me tips on polishing up my emails. I was grateful for all the guidance they provided. The real solution to my problem though, was delivered by Vishen Lakhiani from Mindvalley Insights. And I didn't even know the guy then.

Vishen explained a concept formulated by the legendary advertiser, Eugene Schwartz. After watching his video a couple of times, I went to grab a copy of the book Breakthrough Advertising, in which Schwartz discussed the 5 different sophistication levels of the market. It was not an easy read but once I grasped the concept, I was in awe.

I finally understood why my market wasn't resonating with my marketing and I immediately started rectifying. You see, different audiences are at different sophistication levels. When you market at a lower or higher sophistication level than the level your market is in, your message doesn't get across as smoothly as it should. And this causes your marketing to suffer. The underlying concept has everything to do with psychology. And once I realized this, I became obsessed.

The next few months were spent voraciously devouring every shred of information I could find on the subject. Be it customer psychology, product psychology, copywriting psychology, I would internalize it and apply it on my marketing. I also decided to focus on a new niche (online sales psychology) and began to carve my own space in it. Instead of promoting various affiliate offers to my subscribers, I developed my own training programs and built a pure, new list of subscribers. From over 20,000 subscribers, I was down to less than 400. It was like starting from scratch. But I had never felt better.

This new list was full of life. It gave my business life. It gave me life. The joy I felt (and still feel) while typing an email out to my subscribers was

something I had not felt before. It felt like an engaging conversation between friends. When my subscribers replied to my emails, I felt as though they genuinely knew and understood me. And I guess that resonance came about because I had taken the time to understand them first.

I started to feel like I had found meaning in my work. Like I had found my purpose from my work. Little did I know what an understatement that would be. The psychological competence I had developed did not only enhance my business, it also enhanced my personal relationships. I had unconsciously heightened my empathy towards others and this became a boon when interacting with friends, relatives and even people I would meet for the first time.

I felt I had found my calling in sharing psychology related business tips. But as it would turn out, I was drawn to a higher calling. It all started on a vacation with my partner, Doreen. We were on a tour in Indonesia and our tour guide had brought us to an outdoor go-kart circuit. We were given some time to race around the dirt track before proceeding with the next segment of the tour. I have always enjoyed go-kart racing and I was mentally preparing to clinch first place in the race when Doreen noticed something.

A couple of kids had gathered beside the circuit and were watching the group before ours race. The young children kept their distance and I wasn't sure if they were shy to come closer or if they had been warned by their parents not to come too close. Regardless, they were kids and I could tell they were vicariously enjoying the race. Doreen has a fondness for children and so she told me she wanted to head towards them. With our race starting in just minutes, I was conflicted at first but in the end, I decided to follow her and forfeit the competition.

We hopped on our penny boards and rode down to meet the kids. Instantly, we could see their attention being redirected towards us and they started smiling and pointing at our boards. Perhaps it was their first time seeing these penny boards and they were fascinated. We played with them for a while and although there was a barrier in language, the

interactions we had while letting them try our penny boards more than compensated for it. We shared the language of enjoyment.

One kid in particular made an impression on me. It was an 8 year old boy by the name of Adi. The children were taking turns to ride the penny boards but when it came to Adi's turn, he took his younger sister by the hand, helped her to sit of the board and gently pushed it for her. It was a beautiful scene that really touched us and we decided to give them the penny boards. The innocent pleasure on the faces of those kids alone made our decision easy.

Ever since that day, every time Doreen and I would travel, we would bring something to give any children we would meet. We have been to various places around Indonesia and Thailand and we would usually bring items like badminton rackets and soccer balls. Items they may not have for themselves. Items they should be able to play with as kids.

It's only a small gesture on our part but it brings such happiness to the kids that we make it a point to get the stuff before leaving for our trips. And even though we haven't seen Adi since that day, who knows, perhaps that one encounter may have a ripple effect in the future and he might grow up to spread the love. From what I've seen, I have no doubt he's capable of it.

So far, Doreen and I have only brought toys and sports supplies to share with these kids. But during one of our trips, we learned that some of these kids have to walk over 4 kilometers daily just to attend school. That gave us a long-term idea of building a school in a rural village area so that the children there may have access to education. There is a lot of work to be done to get this idea up and running but I can already tell that Doreen has set her mind on it. Some of the ideas we have bounced off each other include collaborating with some of my corporate clients to bring this idea to fruition. Because who says we can't do business and bring more smiles to the world at the same time.

COMING BACK FROM THE APOCALYPSE

Matt Bacak

I haven't wanted to talk about this before, but in December of 2008 I experienced what my wife, Stephani,e now refers to as "THE APOCALYPSE"...

Basically, my world got turned upside down and I had to start my life again.

I went from being super-successful to dead broke practically overnight, with nothing left to invest in any new business, and no enterprise to fall back on. I was wounded and shell-shocked, but somehow I had to start over – from scratch.

So for the next two years, that's what I did. I needed to generate some income quickly, so I started using the web site ClickBank to market other people's products on line.

Don't worry if you've never heard of ClickBank – I'll be showing you how to make it one of your best revenue sources in just a few minutes. For now let's just say it's like a big, wholesale warehouse that that provides you with countless products and information sources that you can market on line in return for half the revenue you generate.

So using my background in Internet marketing, I gradually crawled out of the hole I'd been shoved into, until, after a few months, I was back earning a good living.

The problem was, I wasn't happy, and I wasn't fulfilled. I still felt angry and victimized by what had happened.

And more than that, after two years of marketing other people's products and information, I realized I desperately wanted something of my own to offer, the way I had done in the past.

I know you're all here because you want to learn how to increase your income, to provide a better life for yourselves and your families. But I also know that your greatest professional satisfaction comes when your knowledge and expertise can touch and benefit as many people as possible.

That's exactly how I felt. I wanted to create a product of my own that would exponentially increase the number of people whose lives I could transform.

In short, I NEEDED A WIN. I had to do something big and audacious, something that had such a high level of success that I knew I was back on top. I wanted to change the rules of Internet marketing.

I started by creating a brand new product – a downloadable set of four, 2-hour videos I called the MASS MONEY MAKERS METHOD. This information, which grew out of my years of experience at the bleeding edge of Internet marketing, would enable anyone to generate Google 1st page keywords, and then use those to create huge contact lists resulting in massive amounts of money.

I knew this information was unique, powerful and effective, and could truly allow anyone to come online and make money with relative ease. The challenge was to generate awareness of the product to an unheard of number of affiliates - people who would promote the product to their own lists for a share of the revenue.

ClickBank has a designation they refer to as GRAVITY. It's a measure of how popular a product is with affiliates. Simply put, every single affiliate who sells a product counts as a gravity rating of 1 for that product. So if 10 different people are selling your product on any given day, its gravity for that day is 10.

The average product offered on ClickBank would have a gravity rating somewhere around 10 or 15. For a new product with a VERY successful launch, the gravity might reach as much as 500. But before I launched Mass Money Makers, only 4 people in the world had ever reached a gravity of 1000. So I declared that when I released my package, it was going to achieve a gravity of 2000.

Remember, I said I had to achieve an unheard of level of success to really believe I was back on top.

I also had my own personal record I was determined to break. In my entire career the most successful launch I had ever achieved – which is still considered a huge success – was 15,000 sales. So I decided Mass Money Makers had to reach 20,000 SALES IN A SINGLE WEEK.

And finally, even though everyone says that the holidays are the WORST possible time to launch a new product, I set mine for December 28TH of 2010. December 31st is my birthday – and celebrating the success of this launch was going to be the start of my new life.

So with the product in place, my goals clear and the launch date set, I began my campaign to create an unheard of level of awareness and anticipation.

I knew achieving the impossible was going to be a huge battle, so I began reading The Art of War. And I decided I was going to amass my own army.

I contacted all the experts whose material I had been marketing for the last two years, told them about my new product, and asked them if they would be willing to pass my promotional material on to their own affiliates, just as a favor to me. They said, "You've been promoting my stuff for the last 2 years, and you've never asked for anything. So of course I'll be glad to help."

Then word started to spread, and by the time of the launch we had 7,551 affiliates marketing my material.

SO WHAT WERE THE RESULTS?

By December 30th, the day before the launch, the phrase MASS MONEY MAKERS had generated more than 125,000 web searches.

By the end of the campaign, it had appeared on 9 MILLION web sites.

On the day of the launch, Alexa, a web site that calculates the most popular topics on the web, ranked Mass Money Makers #1 – ahead of Angelina Jolie and Jennifer Anniston. #4 on the list was the phrase "New Years." We actually outscored New Years ON New Years.

And remember my goal of reaching a Gravity of 2,000 on ClickBank? On January 10th, 2011, we hit 2,086. It remains the highest gravity rating every recorded on ClickBank.

And that goal of selling 20,000 units in a single week? We did it – IN THE FIRST DAY. By the end of the first week, we had sold more than 30,000.

But most important to me was the fact that tens of thousands of people continue to benefit from that program.

And as I had always hoped, when the launch was finished I was able to say, "I won. And I'm back on top."

I know you want to know exactly HOW I did all this. And how you can follow the same steps I did to reach a massive number of people with your products and ideas.

That's what I'm about to tell you. But the story isn't quite over.

Shortly after our record-breaking launch, I got a call from Dan Kennedy and Bill Glazer, two of the most highly respected names in the world of Internet marketing. They said, "We want to lock you in a room for two days with our very best customers, so you can show them step by step how you accomplished the impossible."

They gathered 500 of their top affiliates and charged them $2000 a piece to attend.

Then they recorded my presentation, compiled all my ideas, all my information and all my insider secrets and assembled it into SUPER AFFILIATE SECRETS, a single package of DVDs, CDs, workbooks and bonus materials.

Since you bought this book and helped out on making Everyday Heroes a best seller I wanted to reward you by giving you this link to get it digitally for free.

Simply type this into your browser:

http://everydayheroesbook.com/1k

.

ABOUT THE AUTHORS

Matt Bacak
MattBacak.com

Matt Bacak is considered by many an Internet Marketing Legend. Using his stealth marketing techniques, he became a Best Selling author with a huge fan base of over 1.2 million people in his niche as well as built multi-million dollar companies. After being crowned, 2010 Internet Marketer of the Year, he was asked to appear on National Television, his Lifetime television segment focused on "how to make money using the Internet. The real way". Matt is not only a sought-after internet marketer but has also marketed for some of the world's top experts whose reputations would shrivel if their followers ever found out someone else coached them on their online marketing strategies.

Alex Arnold
TurnThingsAround.net

Alex Arnold, like many people, perhaps even like YOU has enjoyed his fair share of 'ups' and 'downs' in life… However as Alex often says, "It's how we handle the ups and downs of the Roller Coaster of life that really matters… and this is why I'm dedicated to help as many people as possible to turn their life around when they hit rock bottom, just like I know I did." If you've ever dreamed of turning your life around and breaking free from a depressing 9-5 mundane existence and starting your own freedom and lifestyle business instead then you're invited to visit Alex's official website to discover tips to help you turn your life around with fresh thinking as well as ways to improving your health, fitness and wellbeing.

David Asarnow

DavidAsarnow.com

David Asarnow is the founder of Business Oxygen, and How To Monetize business marketing and monetization agencies. He is an authority in monetizing your business. David's clients have added millions of dollars to their bottom line after implementing David's business monetization strategies. David has trained thousands of business professionals worldwide, including those for clients like Tony Robbins and Chet Holmes Business Breakthroughs International. Some of David's clients have included Coca-Cola, International Paper, McDonalds, Sam's Club, Wal-Mart, Costco, Dairy Queen. David's personal passions are his family, Crossfit and the outdoors.

Benjamin Bressington
BenBressington.com

Benjamin Bressington is known as "Mr. Gamification" by Fox News. Benjamin's specialty is customer engagement and applying the principles and addictive nature of games to business. Benjamin has consulted with multi-Billion dollar companies to create their mobile marketing strategies along with publishing over 300 Apps. As the author of multiple books Benjamin's companies focus on helping business owners and entrepreneurs engage their customers to improve lead generation, sales and conversions. Benjamin focuses on creating marketing strategies around existing human behaviors to piggy back existing habits.

Lou Brown
StreetSmartInvestor.com

Investors have long regarded the training, systems and forms created by Louis "Lou" Brown as the best in the industry. Quoted as an expert by many publications such as *The Wall Street Journal* and *Smart Money,* Lou draws from his wide and varied background as a real estate investor. Having bought property since 1977, he has invested in single-family homes, apartments, hotels and developed subdivisions, as well as building and renovating homes and apartments. These experiences have given him a proving ground for the most cutting edge concepts in the real estate investment industry today. He is widely known as a creative financing genius regarding his deal structuring concepts. He enjoys sharing his discoveries with others as he teaches seminars and has authored courses, books and audio training on how to make money and keep it.

Milton Brown
FullChargeMarketing.com

Milton is life-long resident of North Carolina, where he resides with his loving wife and beautiful daughter. He created and earned his NCSU Bachelors in Adolescent Development. Through his love of knowledge, he began to learn and teach himself the secrets of Digital Marketing. Through his efforts and careful guidance of his mentor, Matt Bacak, Milton Brown is now the Vice President & Agency Partner of Full Charge Marketing. Milton Brown also has a passion for helping children accomplish success and realize their true potential. Through this passion he and his family created the non-profit, Prosperous Living Achievement Center (PLAC), to reach this goal. PLAC focuses on working with low income, at-risk youth. Their program has a strong Math and Reading based program. They also provide character and leadership building classes to help the youth become successful in every area of their life.

Ani Catino
InternetInspirations.net

Ani is considered a good friend, good listener and special person. But just thinks of herself as an ordinary mum to two boys, a wife, a sister and a daughter in a friendly little town. Born in Turkey, to an Armenian mother and an Italian father, she speaks four languages and that made her decide to become an interpreter/translator for the past fifteen years where one day is never the same to the next.

She considers herself one of the lucky people to enjoy her work while doing a lot of travelling and meeting new people as well as working at her own pace. Ani's passion though is, running her own business. In order to be successful, I educate and self-develop myself from other people's experiences, ideas and knowledge by learning from them. Nevertheless, as my family is very important to me, I have to make the time for them. I don't think any amount of money would replace the loss time, if you don't enjoy with the people you love and appreciate their existence.

Tom Cone
MemberGate.com

Tom Cone is the CEO of MemberGate a class leading membership and subscription software company. He owns and runs several subscription sites and has over ten years, hands-on experience of researching, launching, operating, growing those sites into autopilot businesses which have serviced thousands of members and returned several million dollars. For exclusive access to "32 Topic Ideas for Subscription Web Sites" and software to calculate the 'Profit Potential' of your subscription web-site idea, go to":
www.MemberGate.com/superhero

Diane Conklin

CompleteMarketingSystems.com

Diane Conklin is an internationally known author, entrepreneur, coach, consultant, marketing and business strategist, implementation specialist and speaker. Diane is a direct response marketing expert who specializes in showing business owners how to integrate their online and offline marketing strategies, media and message, to get maximum results from their marketing dollars.

For more than 17 years Diane has been leading small businesses to bigger profits through her proprietary home study systems, speaking from the platform and by providing done-for-you services to clients all over the world.

As the founder of Complete Marketing Systems and the LGBT Success Academy, Diane and has been involved in numerous campaigns grossing over $1,000,000.00 several times in her career and routinely helps people grow businesses to 6 figures, and beyond, in short periods of time, several times in as little as 90 days.

Diane was voted Glazer-Kennedy Marketer of the Year for her innovative marketing strategies and campaigns and was nominated for Atlanta Business Woman of the Year.

Rosanne D'Ausilio, PhD

Human-Technologies.com

Rosanne D'Ausilio, PhD, is an industrial psychologist, consultant, master trainer, bestselling author, executive coach, keynote speaker, customer service expert, and President of Human Technologies Global.

She is known as the 'practical champion for the human' and authors 14+ best sellers: Wake Up Your Call Center: Humanize Your Interaction Hub, 4th ed, Customer Service and the Human Experience, Lay Your Cards on the Table: 52 Ways to Stack Your Personal Deck (includes 32-card deck), How to Kick Your Customer Service

Up A Notch: 101 Insider Tips, Vol I and II, the Expert's Guide to Customer Service, Vol I and II, books on Kindle as well as Create Space (the paperback edition of Amazon), as well as a popular complimentary 'tips' newsletter on How To Kick Your Customer Service Up A Notch! at www.HumanTechTips.com

She represents the human element on the Advisory Board of an Italian software company, authors numerous articles for industry newsletters, and is a much sought after dynamic, vibrant, internationally prominent keynote speaker.

Her main site is www.human-technologies.com and she can be reached at Rosanne@human-technologies.com She has offices in Northern Virginia and the Dominican Republic (in the Winter months)

Suzanne Edwards

Human-Technologies.com

Suzanne graduated in London with a degree in Communication and Media Production. She worked for many large blue chip global companies working with Senior Management and Board Directors. She contributed towards moving a small business to a medium sized business and now works for herself at Little Big Leaders providing Reading and Writing for children from the age of 3.5 and giving children aged 5 to 11 the opportunity to better enhance their Math and English with the aim of many gaining entry into some of the most prestigious school in London. Currently, she runs three tutoring centres with scope for more. The skills acquired while working in some for the largest blue chip companies she applies to her our business and currently obtaining some great results. Many clients return year after year with other siblings or family members. Suzanne undertakes many speaking engagements and looking forward to taking her business to the next level. She attends many professional development courses and applies the knowledge to develop her business. She is looking forward to developing a world-class business.

Brian T. Evans Jr.
BrianEvansJr.com

Brian T. Evans Jr., is an Award Winning Entrepreneur - 2015 Marketer of the Year; 2-time Best Selling Author; Business & Marketing Consultant & Real Estate Investing Expert. He has been interviewed on local news channels such as Fox, NBC, & CBS discussing his businesses and entrepreneurial experiences.

Sharvin Exubrio
SharvinExubrio.com

Why are my ads losing money? That's a question Sharvin is asked a lot. As the founder of Online Entrepreneurs Hub, Sharvin teaches online entrepreneurs how to create marketing messages that lead to the sale. His core ideology focuses on understanding the silent thoughts customers have when considering a purchase. While analyzing his winning sales messages, Sharvin realized that there are 67 questions every marketer needs to answer first before even starting a marketing campaign. These 67 questions form the basis of his customer avatar checklist, which he calls "The Crystal Ball." Sharvin has tested The Crystal Ball across various industries and the questions reveal so much about the customer's core desires that some customers have even declared that Sharvin understood their needs even better than they did. With The Crystal Ball, Sharvin has helped new marketers with no experience in advertising launch successful campaigns. He has helped experienced marketers change their losing campaigns, which they had to constantly pause, into winning ones. He has also helped his corporate clients boost their marketing ROI by over 280%. Be the first person your customer thinks of when deciding to buy.

Eileen Forrestal
EileenForrestal.com

"You are the source of your own wellbeing and happiness. You have everything you need inside you to be the best you can be." Eileen Forrestal Eileen's life demonstrates that when change happens and you see the open door, and you step through it, your life can be better than you imagined. "The cave you fear to enter holds the treasure you seek." (Joseph Campbell). After 25 years as a medical doctor, she literally walked up to a door and a wild and wonderful opportunity opened up.

Eileen's is a remarkable story in the example it provides of overcoming obstacles, 'surviving' emotional stress, seizing opportunity, courageously re-inventing her life and now thriving with freedom and ease.

in 2014, Eileen gave up her career in medicine, and decided that she can do more, for people, with products and services that uplift, educate, inspire, and empower people to be at the source of their own health, well being and happiness.

She has re-invented herself and her life, and believes that she can inspire and encourage others do the same. Forgive the past - live the present - create the future.

About the Authors

Kathleen Gage
KathleenGage.com

Kathleen Gage has a *Passion for Thriving*. As an award winning speaker, writing and business owner, Kathleen is known as the "no-nonsense, common sense" online marketing strategist, speaker, author, product creation specialist, and owner of Power Up For Profits. She helps experts grow their businesses by being highly visible to their market by writing books, speaking on the platform and committing to a life of playing full out.

Kathleen speaks, writes, consults and teaches about what she believes are the core elements of a successful life: accountability, integrity, honesty, and living with passion and hope. When Kathleen is not working with clients, creating information products, writing books or speaking on the platform, Kathleen can be found sharing time with her life partner of 27 years, Karen; training and participating in foot races, walking her dogs, working in her many flower gardens, feeding her horses or playing a fierce game of cards. One of her "bucket-list" goals is to run 100 races (5k's, 10's, 5 & 10 miles, and half marathons) by the time she turns 70 – only a few short years away.

Henry Gold
HenryGoldTips.com

Henry is recognized as the "#1 Digital Product Launch Expert for Anyone Who Wants to Make Big Money Selling Their Own Digital Product on the Internet!"

He has been instrumental to the launching of digital products in social media of not only many small and medium businesses but also of some from the self-improvement, health and wellness industries as well.

Henry is a sought after copywriter, product launch strategist and International Speaker. He has published more than a hundred digital products, and worked with best-selling authors, celebrities, and movie producers. In fact, he was an integral part of the mastermind group of some of the most intelligent marketers in the world.

Mr. Gold owns three businesses, has read and researched over a thousand books on leadership and marketing and has a network with over 3,000 entrepreneurs across the globe.

Deanna Grayly
DeannaGraylyOnline@gmail.com

Deanna was born in Liverpool in the U.K. She missed an opportunity to meet her heroes, the pop group known as the Beatles. A small number of people at her high school were invited to meet the Beatles at the Town Hall. The School Principal kept the numbers down by catching anyone chatting in the morning assembly. So Deanna and a few others missed out.

Since then Deanna has done her best not to miss another fantastic opportunity. Deanna believes one cannot put a price on good health and the love of close family and friends. Deanna has learned not to take anything or anyone for granted and loves it when a business project works out well.

Deanna is currently working on a project regarding how to help diabetics stay focused and healthy.

Chris Hickman
GetBackOnGoogle.com

Chris Hickman is the Founder and CEO at Adficient with 14 years of experience in search marketing and 9 years with Adwords policy compliance. He founded Adficient to help people with PPC and SEO who have had a bad experience in the past. He also founded GetBackOnGoogle.com to help businesses get back on Google. Chris loves listening to audiobooks on self-improvement business skills. There are people who can spend 30 years mastering something and put it into a book and charge you $10 or $20. To Chris, you cannot find a better deal than this. A few times a year you can see him at Keystone skiing down the mountain trying to break his current speed record of 54.9 mph.

Daryl Hill
Linkedin.com/in/Daryl Hill

Daryl started his entrepreneurial career at the age of 7, when he asked for a toy that his mom said she was not going to buy. After earning enough to buy the toy himself, he learned that anything in life was possible, and overcoming challenges would become a way of life for him. Overcoming severe learning disabilities, he channeled his energy into sports where he excelled to become a three-year starter for the Naval Academy Football team. Upon graduation, he chose the US Marine Corps where he rose to the rank of Major. He enlisted to become an Infantry Officer and he led Marines into Combat Operations overseas.

After leaving the Marine Corps he carved out a professional niche career by developing a process to help people overcome limited beliefs inside their minds that prevent them from achieving their full potential. He currently works with enlightened entrepreneurs (Daryl labels "wounded sheepdogs") that have hit a mental barrier when looking for the next step in their careers. He also works with professional athletes who want to discover and go to the next level in their prospective sports careers.

His true passion is helping veterans with the invisible scars of war called post-traumatic stress disorder (PTSD). He is constantly looking for ways to help them achieve personal goals and overcome the mental obstacles caused by PTSD.

Nick James
InternetMarketingTrainingClub.com

From humble beginnings working as a lowly paid parking lot attendant, Nick James is now widely considered one of the World's leading Internet Marketing consultants and has recently been awarded Internet Marketer of the Year 2016 by the professional marketers peer group The Profit Coalition.

He's been invited to make keynote presentations on stage at some of the world's most prestigious business marketing seminars, such as the Entrepreneur's Bootcamp in the UK and the Digital Marketing Summit. He's been interviewed by some of the most successful marketers in the world, such as Matt Bacak, Shawn Casey and the legendary Ted Nicholas. Just to name a few.

His BuildMyListNow.net list-building program is getting rave reviews from seasoned Internet Marketers as well as from college students, stay-at-home moms and retired grandparents. In the BuildMyListNow.net system he outlines a step-by-step plan that is simple to follow, yet incredibly powerful when it comes to generating new leads for any business.

If you would like to discover the 'new rules' for generating fresh daily leads and building a constantly growing list of new email subscribers, then simply send a quick email to EverydayHeros@Nick-James.co.uk and he will send you full details of the system he developed. The system that ended up winning him Internet Marketer of the Year 2016 because of his unique new angle on list building.

Jocelyn Jones
Jrlive.net

Jocelyn Jones AKA The Instagram Mama, is an Instagram Marketing Expert, International Speaker, and Online Marketing Consultant. She shows you how to have Success through Socializing. Most recent Speaking Tour involves The Social Media Summit at The Grand Lucayan in Freeport, Grand Bahama, Dubai, Bahrain and Pakistan. She has been featured on ZNS TV and Radio, KISS FM, The Bahamas Weekly, Bahrain This Month, The Ask Bon Bon Show, TV and Radio in both Dubai and Bahrain, Business Plus TV in Pakistan, The BottomLine Live Show out of Los Angeles, and The Jennings Wire Podcast. Her Simple 3 Step Formula teaches you how to Attract Followers, Build Your List and Convert them to Customers in as little as 15 minutes a day, allowing you more time to do the things you love.

About Paul Kelly
how2alkalise.com

Paul J Kelly is from Strabane, Co Tyrone in Northern Ireland and is married to Lorraine. He has a teenage son, Jason. I sell Asea Water and water machines to help others stay healthy.

Since getting involved in the business of health and wealth, I have travelled extensively to promote what I believe in. Places I have had the opportunity to visit include London, Barcelona, New York, Las Vegas and Kenya to name a few. I put in many hours of work each week. I attend lots of seminars and events to broaden my knowledge with the bonus of making new contacts on each occasion. I also have invested in quite a few coaches for both my personal and business development.

My personal mantra is inspired by Richard Branson. He said – "If someone offers you an amazing opportunity, say yes and work out how to do it later! So, what are you waiting for? Change your water and change your life"

Donna Kennedy
DonnaKennedy.com

Donna Kennedy is a three-time best selling author, with *The Confidence to Succeed* being her most recent release. She is a qualified psychologist, life coach, business coach and mentor. Her academic work has been published nationally and internationally by various faculties, including *The American Journal of Psychology* and *The Irish Psychological Record*. She has been endorsed by world leading organizations and has worked with many personal development leaders, including Bob Proctor (*The Secret*), Mark Victor-Hansen (*Chicken Soup for The Soul*), Brian Tracy (CEO of *Brian Tracy International*), Sharon Lechter (*Think and Grow Rich for Women* and *Rich Dad, Poor Dad*), *Anthony Robbins Foundation*. Donna regularly features in national and international media as an expert in the areas of personal and business development.

Donna experienced several challenges in her early years but overcame those challenges against all odds. At one point in her life her confidence was so low that she was afraid to walk across the street on her own. Now she is a confident woman who says yes to life and embraces opportunity.

Having learned from some of the world's greatest achievers, at age 23 she bought her first investment property and at age 24 she created her first company, turning over a €1,000,000 in the first year. Year-on-year she has gone from strength to strength and is impacting people worldwide with her fresh and unique approach. If you want better results in your life and business, learn from Donna

Gary Kissel
Linkedin.com/in/GaryKissel

Gary Kissel is a global LinkedIn strategist, author and speaker. LinkedIn selected him as a <u>Profinder</u> in the Marketing Consultant category and recommends Gary as a highly qualified contact to those who seek help with their business marketing. As a Realtor Gary used LinkedIn to find, connect and do deals with investors around the world.

As a LinkedIn expert Gary is ranked in the Top 1% for his industry, Professional Training & Coaching. Gary is also active on Twitter and has the distinction as the #1 LinkedIn Strategist on that platform. He is followed by nearly 50,000 in the "Twitterverse". Gary has published over 20 articles on LinkedIn and he has an eBook entitled, "Vital LinkedIn Tips: How to Make Money on LinkedIn Now". He was a contributor to LinkedIn's 2014 eBook entitled, "Getting Started with Social Selling on LinkedIn".Most recently, Gary is a contributing author to a soon-to-be-released book with Matt Bacak, one of the world's top internet marketers, and others entitled "Everyday Heroes". He has realized success for himself because he puts his clients' success first."Giving back" is important to Gary and he does so by supporting organizations such as Habitat for Humanity.

Tony McCarthy
Facebook.com/AnthonyMcCarthy

Anthony is a family man and proud husband and father of five. After many years of owning retail showrooms and construction contracting, he moved home to an office I his back garden and starting working full time on the internet. The reason, to have more time with his family. Tired of the daily grind, Anthony wanted and found a better way of life.

Anthony's businesses have generated tens of millions of dollars and now with over three decades of offline and online marketing experience, he brings a wealth of practical experience to the new age of marketing. Known among his marketing peers as "Mr Mobile" or "The Mobile Guy", he has taught numerous businesses and start-ups how to market their business.

He has been called upon by government ministers to speak about the internet, has been a government mentor, collage lecturer on the topics of mobile marketing and online marketing. He is a director of numerous companies and owns Adapptise Ltd a company that has received a grant for its cutting edge disruptive software from Horizon 20/20.

Anthony's no hold barred, no nonsense style has set him apart and he has spoken around the world on the topic of mobile, social media and online marketing. He believes that marketing your business in today's world means you understand all the different "touch points" with your market and explains how you can capitalise on a multi-screen world

Lee Nazal
ClientsInAdvance.com

Lee Nazal is a Marketing Strategist who literally wrote the book on high response lead generation and prospecting for B2B entrepreneurs. His Amazon best-selling book, called "APPROACH," is the definitive guide to cold email outreach prospecting. Over the past decade, he's generated millions of dollars in revenue for his clients. He also trains online entrepreneurs, digital marketers, and local and offline consultants on generating leads and converting them into high-ticket sales. Because of the guidance he received during a low point in his career and personal life, he has made it his mission to help entrepreneurs become as successful as possible with their businesses so that they, too, can change the trajectory of someone who struggled as he once did. He does this by helping marketers that find difficulty in standing out in a crowded marketplace to attract high-paying clients, close more deals, eliminate competition, and generate monthly Reliable Revenue for their businesses. Lee lives in Atlanta with his beautiful wife and three amazing children.

David Perdew
MyNams.com

David Perdew, CEO and founder of NAMS - the Novice to Advanced Marketing System. He's a journalist, consultant and serial entrepreneur who has built one of the most successful and fastest growing business training systems online today called the MyNAMS Insiders Club.

The Novice to Advanced Marketing System is a step-by-step system focusing on Team, Training and Tools to help novice to advanced business people build a Simple, Scalable and Sustainable business.

He took a year off in 2003 to personally build a 2200 square foot log cabin in north Alabama where he and his wife and two dogs and a cat live on 95 acres of forest with four streams and a 60-foot waterfall.

Phil Perrin
Facebook.com/Philip.Perrin.507

Phil Perrin is a confident, versatile and enthusiastic coach experienced in training developing and leading teams. Motivating and mentoring business owners to measure and take proactive actions, to increase both profit and growth. His focus is typically in one of 11 areas: Profit, Cash-flow Marketing, Sales, Strategy, Teams, Innovation, Systems, Teamwork, Operational Excellence and Time Management. Always passionate about helping others, working to the highest standards and creating win-win scenarios.

Jill Niemen-Picerno
PureJill.net

Jill Niemen-Picerno is a professional network marketer and home-based business coach. Her passion for helping people have success of their own in all aspects related to network marketing and/or owning a business from the comfort of their home can be felt from the first time you talk with her. She has been interviewed, by Doug Llewelyn on "Moving America Forward", a television series that highlights the achievements and spirit of entrepreneurs and businesses across America. During her interview, she spoke about her PURE Coaching Program, "**P**owerfully **U**nleashing the **R**eal **E**ntrepreneur in you". In an interview by Gary Atencio, on Consumer News Television series, where consumers tune in and trust CNTV to introduce the Best of Colorado. Here she spoke about her success in the industry and her love of this business model to help people change their lives. In fact, this love led Jill to co-created a song called "Livin the Dream" about it. See iTunes.

Sherman Ragland
dcreia.com

Sherman Ragland, CCIM recently named by Inc. Magazine as "America's Real Estate Mentor" is the Dean of the Realinvestors' Academy (based just outside Washington, DC) and Chief Visionary for Realinvestors' Online University, REIU. Sherman is known for helping more people to successfully get into real estate investing in the DC Region than any other Mentor. "Donald Trump Could Learn A Great Deal From Sherman Ragland!", says Apprentice Star Kristi Frank. He is the Host of Real Investors™ Talk Radio.com, a program dedicated to assisting people in all walks of life to learn the correct way to invest in real estate. He is the Founder of DC-REIA.COM, the Greater Washington, DC Real Estate Investors' Association www.dcreia.com, the largest and most successful real estate training organization in the DC/No Va./Central Md. region.

Pat Slattery
PatSlattery.com

Pat Slattery is no ordinary speaker or coach, leaving school at 14yrs old he began working and by having an incredibly positive attitude and outstanding work ethic along with his determination to give 100% to everything he does, Pat went on to build his security business to a point where it turned over €25,000,000, he has successfully brought other companies to the level where they have generated millions of euro. Pats talks come straight from the heart, the ups and downs of business and life experiences, Pat gives practical information that he has applied himself that has driven him to the successes he has achieved in his life and business. He speaks to corporate and public audiences on the subjects of Personal and Professional Development, including the executives and staff of many of many large companies and organizations.. He has mentored thousands of people across many different types of businesses. Pat is known internationally as a business strategist and has facilitated growth in many companies and entrepreneurs that has brought their life and business to extraordinary levels

Paul Wakefield
Paul-Wakefield.co.uk

I'm exceptionally good at being a lifestyle coach. I've been changing and improving lives since 1997. (Sorry too many people try to be modest about what they're good at... I don't know why. I've been inspiring, supporting and helping people since I was 20 years old. I was first booked to talk to 35 students at Amersham & Wycombe College in my home town when I was 20 years old. Since then I've learned more, experienced more, failed more and succeeded in more, I've gotten better. So that means, I'm really good and I'm not shy about it; if you're exceptional at something, you shouldn't be either.) I'm very driven. I'm tough and blunt. (I'm tough and blunt because people come to me with a destination they want to get too, but they've never been. So I have to be. Weak people shouldn't call, email or sign-up or listen to anything I print, deliver or discuss.) I'm launching my own menswear clothing range called Paul Wakefield Clothing. I'm a published author with a book on sale in 27 different countries.

I'm a man sharing his journey with the world

David Wright

Atlantaseos.com/press/

David B. Wright is a bestselling author and is President of W3 Group Marketing, a marketing firm that helps growth-oriented businesses get more customers, patients and clients. David provides marketing services ranging from high-level strategic direction down to the tactical implementation including SEO, video marketing, online advertising, online reputation management, mobile, local, social, online PR, and more. Video SEO is a particular sweet spot - David has gotten to Page One of Google in as fast as thirty-six seconds! He also won "Best Local Author" in Creative Loafing's Best of Atlanta 2016 awards. David is an international speaker, has lived in Tokyo, Japan, done business around the world and has been quoted in numerous publications including Inc. Magazine, The Wall Street Journal, CNN, AMEX Open Forum, About.com, and Business Insider. He has climbed Mt. Fuji and dozens of other mountains, loves SCUBA diving, kayaking, music and all sorts of adventures. He is a champion fish taco chef, learned to surf in Bali, shot archery in the crater of a Japanese volcano, was a radio DJ in Atlanta, rode an elephant through the jungle in Thailand, and is ready for his next adventure together with his wife and daughter.

Dushka Zapata
Linkedin.com/in/Dushka

After more than 20 years in the communications industry I noticed a theme. It is very difficult to articulate who you are and what you do. This holds true for both companies and for individuals. For companies, this is an impediment to the development of an identity, a reputation, a brand. It makes it hard for your customers to see how you are different from your competitors. For individuals, in a new world order of personal brands, it makes it hard to develop one that feels real. This is what I do. I help companies and people put into simple terms who they are, what they do, and where to go next. I help people identify why they are stuck and how to get un-stuck. My work comes to life through message development, presentation training, media training and personal brand development. It comes to life through executive coaching, workshops and public speaking. It comes to life through what I write. I published a book last May called How to be Ferociously Happy.

Helga Zelinski
Facebook.com/Helga.Zelinski

Helga Zelinski was born in Germany and immigrated to Canada with her family in the 1960's. She studied and worked in the Natural Health field and has many years of clinical experience in the prevention and treatment of obesity and weight loss. She is the author of several books with the focus on digestive functions, micro-organisms and human behavior. Her passion is to share some of the facts which relate to making better decisions in general and changing old habits in particular. Better choices to improve the quality of life

On behalf of all authors in this book, thank you again for getting Everyday Heroes. Remember, 100% of ALL royalties for this book will be donated to Children's Healthcare Of Atlanta, because the Children are the real heroes of the future!

"YOUR SPECIAL BONUS LINK"

Digital Marketing Legend, Matt Bacak included a website link INSIDE the last chapter of this book, which provides you with downloadable access to a digital marketing training course valued at $1,000.

In the past, this course was only sold at GKIC (Glazer Kennedy Insiders Circle) events for $1,000, but Matt is giving it away for free because you have your hands on this book.

You will find this special link on <u>page 144</u>

Go right now and grab it!

Made in the USA
Lexington, KY
11 November 2016